Hystericizing Germany

Hys志cizing Germany
Fassbinder, Alexanderplatz

Manfred Hermes

Sternberg Press

Contents

Not Everything Takes Place within a Single Continuity or Frame of Reference 7

The Themes Are (Not) There for the Taking 17

Nuances of Modernity 45

Using Machines to Make This Peculiar Thing We Call an Image 65

Which Social Perspective, and How? 79

Kinks in the Historical 111

On the Stage of Maximum Ambiguity 137

Arc de cercle 163

Supplements

- Berlin, Super-City 171
- German Calamities (1980–2010) 175
- Jewish Matters: Appropriation of Tradition 189
- Jewish Matters: *Garbage, the City, and Death* 195
- Jewish Matters: Representation 201
- *Tales of a Long Night* 209
- Exhibiting a Movie 215

Index 219

Not Everything Takes Place within a Single Continuity or Frame of Reference

Rainer Werner Fassbinder once described the difference in impact between cinema and television as follows: “It sounds idiotic if I say I want to popularize Freud, that television performs a psychoanalytical function. I think it’s easier to resist in the cinema, because you’re sitting in a public space among strangers, whereas when you watch television you’re sitting with your family … that’s where things really start to get interesting.”[1]

If *Berlin Alexanderplatz* was meant to have such an impact, I certainly didn’t notice at the time, as I was largely indifferent to most of Fassbinder’s films. I don’t want to write a bildungsroman here, or a story of sudden revelations. But sometimes it’s good to take stock of how, when, and why one’s judgments began to change. In my case, the earliest pointers were small things: decor details, particular body/camera correlations, a fashion sense, the “double blackface” of Günther Kaufmann’s African-American mother in *Whity* (1971), the statesmanlike tirades and racist graffiti copied into the frame of *The Third*

1 Rainer Werner Fassbinder, interview by Christian Braad Thomsen (1977), in *Fassbinder über Fassbinder: Die ungekürzten Interviews*, ed. Robert Fischer (Frankfurt am Main: Verlag der Autoren, 2004), 402.

Generation (1979).[2] Even a simple dedication, as in the opening credits of *Querelle* (1982), can open up a space full of implications: "This film is dedicated to my friendship with El Hedi ben Salem m'Barek Mohammed Mustafa. Rainer Werner Fassbinder."

Scattered highlights or compelling aspects do not add up to a full picture, but, as I said, they can act as pointers. In part, my indifference may also have been due to the uneven appeal of Fassbinder's films. His oeuvre is patchy, many films are sloppily made, few are truly accomplished—if by accomplishment one means that all of the elements presented are successfully subsumed under a single principle (possible exceptions include *Satan's Brew*, *Effi Briest*, and *Veronika Voss*). Certain standards like tight exposition and dénouement, chase and fight scenes, or a conventional dramatic arc are fulfilled almost unwillingly. But although he was no action specialist, although his films are rarely sidesplittingly funny, and although his technique tends toward complication in every respect, there is a succinct satirical humor at work here; there is great intensity and tension. Fassbinder's films can even be "touching," no matter how distant they sometimes seem. All of them feature the enchanting and the repulsive, sentimentality and wisdom, the obscene and the sublime, often in quick succession. Because he largely avoided clichés and shock tactics, his work may take longer to warm to, especially in the case of these less-than-perfect films.

2 The statement in question was made by Helmut Schmidt with reference to an operation carried out in violation of Germany's constitution by the country's paramilitary police unit GSG9—an operation Schmidt himself had ordered to free the *Landshut*, a Lufthansa airliner hijacked and flown to Mogadishu in 1977. The flashing intertitle reads as follows: "'I can only thank the German legal profession for not checking the whole thing [meaning the Mogadishu operation, and perhaps other related matters?] with regard to constitutional law.' Helmut Schmidt, serving chancellor of the Federal Republic of Germany, speaking to news weekly *Der Spiegel*, printed in its issue of January 15, 1979."

But even in the less-accomplished or hastily made works (*Whity*, *Lola*) there are many moments that stick in one's mind, where something clicks. A case in point is *Rio das Mortes* (1971). Two friends want to change their lives and abandon their jobs to seek hidden treasure in Peru. They try to save up, counting and recounting their pennies. But the dream has to be postponed. A female friend says they should be more realistic, advising them to lure financial backers with a project that sounds halfway profitable. But even coming up with a fraudulent business plan proves to be hard work. At the library they read up on cotton growing. According to a book from 1871 (!) there are "great prospects!" The German writer and environmental activist Carl Amery, playing a librarian, speaks about budgeting in developing countries: they must adapt to the international division of labor, develop their own markets, tailor their output to the "desired" monocultures. So the young men's longing is directed toward a country where the doctrine of comparative cost advantage has already been in effect for quite some time, not without German involvement. Further disillusionments follow. By the time they set off, the treasure-hunters, their heads in the clouds, have become potential capitalists, ready to be carried away by the film's titular river of death.

In *Rio das Mortes* we see little of the technician of the imaginary that Fassbinder had in fact already become by this time. But in the film's focus on economics, the symbolic order is revealed as the abstract system that is it, multiply interwoven with desire, something he demonstrated in each and every one of his films.

This also means that the tensions present here cannot be reduced to a particular attentiveness to power relations or character structures. In Fassbinder's work, emotions, attitudes, and defects are always just reflex, not purpose. Similarly, we are not dealing with precise portrayals of particular social spheres, although such portrayals do exist in Fassbinder's films. What takes place between people or within groups is not significant in and of itself; even the most disruptive personal disorders have historical and economic aspects. There is something else at stake here. Crucial to Fassbinder's approach was his insistence on staging aporias. Everything in his work is conceived of in terms of violence, trauma, and pain, and this is the weightiest determining factor in a constellation already laden with overdetermination.

In the end, if not from the outset, Fassbinder thus became a historiographer of the German condition and of a specifically German mourning. Expressing this mourning was a function he saw as his own and one that was largely conceded to him by contemporary critics.

Fassbinder's death in 1982 coincided with major changes in German cinema. In the mid-1980s, the discrediting of auteur cinema had begun to bear fruit. German films were now expected to be popular and commercially successful. [German Calamities (1980–2010)]* This may explain why reception of Fassbinder in West Germany came to an almost total standstill around that time. Even in today's Germany, he is famous above all for being famous. Although this ensures that major anniversaries are commemorated, it doesn't secure his films the status of vehicles for thought. More recent reviews show how stereotypes established during Fassbinder's lifetime are still capable of acting as smoke screens. Writers talk about burning the candle at both ends, the despot in his "Munich factory," or melodrama as the genre supposedly at the core of his work.[3] More indestructible

* Titles in square brackets refer to the supplements in the back of the book.

3 Since "melodrama" is and always has been peculiarly associated with Fassbinder, some clarification is called for. That Fassbinder was impressed by Douglas Sirk's films is beyond doubt, and he confirmed it himself often enough. But the manner of this influence did not correspond to the standard version subsequently established by film critics. The following

still is the notion that he made particularly offensive use of his own "subjectivity," "experiences," and foibles as the basis for his films.[4] He is and always has been accused of aestheticism at precisely those points from which it would have been possible to discuss the ideas that went into the work or his particular approach to realism.

Taken together, these various kinds of distortion, disparagement, and false praise add up to little short of a miniaturization. [Exhibiting a Movie] In Germany, the little recognition that was based on sympathy or familiarity with the work came chiefly from within the fields of theater, art, feminist theory, and music. It certainly didn't come from a cinephile German public, and it is hard to say whether this was due to aversion, incapacity, or just Fassbinder-fatigue. (The tide in Germany has turned slightly of late.)

In spite of this, there is a widely held view in Germany that we have been positively inundated with discourse about

dates are important here: in the summer of 1971, the British film magazine *Screen* published a special issue on melodrama; in 1972, a retrospective of twenty Sirk films was shown at the Edinburgh Film Festival; Fassbinder's fascination can be dated to the year 1970. What he learned from Sirk was already put into practice in *The Merchant of Four Seasons* (1971), but perhaps its fullest application came in *Ali: Fear Eats the Soul* (1974). In many other films by Fassbinder, however, melodrama in the usual sense plays no part, neither in *Effi Briest* nor in *The Stationmaster's Wife*, and certainly not in *Berlin Alexanderplatz*. Fassbinder was sometimes confronted in person with this reductionist notion of his absolute and intrinsic dependence on melodrama. On one such occasion, in an interview in 1980 with Wolfgang Limmer and Fritz Rumler, he dismissed the claim: "That's been done to death. I would say that Sirk gave me the courage to make films with mass appeal." Fischer, *Fassbinder über Fassbinder*, 500.

4 The obituary for Fassbinder in *Der Spiegel* (no. 24, 1982) united all of these stereotypes in a single text. After the usual references to his "restless productivity" and "42 films in 13 years," the author also mentioned *Berlin Alexanderplatz*, a work in which Fassbinder "found himself in radical openness. [...] It is true that no Fassbinder film exists that can be talked about without talking about Fassbinder himself. [...] He used the struggle with his own ego as the driving force and raw material for his works." Similar views were to be found in articles accompanying the rerelease of *Berlin Alexanderplatz* in 2007.

Fassbinder's films. In fact, the only significant engagement with his work has taken place in the English-speaking world, especially in the United States.[5] This imbalance in interest levels between America and Germany is odd considering the "German" relevance of Fassbinder's films. But of course, bemoaning this peculiar state of affairs does not form a basis for further engagement.

It is time, then, to explain my object choice. What makes a book, a study, an essay on *Berlin Alexanderplatz* (referred to hereafter as *BA*) so necessary and compelling? And why this limitation to just the one film? To an extent, Fassbinder's series was a special case. He had already made film versions of literary works and created series for television, and he had already developed similar motifs and ideas in feature-length films. But here, behind fourteen leaden episode titles, the sheer amount of material and themes, their meanings passing through so many channels, makes orientation difficult: issues of gender; human/animal contingencies; the ideological function of the media; the welfare state and psychiatry; questions of power, of fate, and of freedom. Even the historical facts of 1929 appear more

5 About *Berlin Alexanderplatz* itself, there are a few pages in Thomas Elsaesser's book on Fassbinder and, as the most ambitious piece, a text by Kaja Silverman, from which Elsaesser borrowed most of his approach. A brief bibliography: Thomas Elsaesser, *Rainer Werner Fassbinder* (Berlin: Bertz + Fischer Verlag, 2001); Kaja Silverman, *Male Subjectivity at the Margins* (New York: Routledge, 1992); Eric Rentschler, "Terms of Dismemberment: The Body in/and/of Fassbinder's *Berlin Alexanderplatz* (1980)," in *German Film and Literature: Adaptations and Transformations*, ed. Eric Rentschler (New York: Methuen, 1986), 305–21; Douglas Crimp, "Fassbinder, Franz, Fox, Elvira, Erwin, Armin, and All the Others," *October*, no. 21 (Summer 1982): 62–81; Richard Dyer, "Reading Fassbinder's Sexual Politics," in *Fassbinder*, ed. Tony Rayns (London: British Film Institute, 1980), 54–64; various other articles and special numbers were devoted to Fassbinder by *October* and *New German Critique*. It must be said, however, that the emphasis has often been on bodies and the "disembodied gaze." For a more recent academic endeavor, see Brigitte Peucker, ed., *A Companion to Rainer Werner Fassbinder* (Malden, MA: Wiley-Blackwell, 2012).

topical today than they can possibly have been in 1980 (crisis of parliamentarianism, high unemployment, organized crime as an irreducible economic factor).

But in *BA*, as well as raising issues and addressing themes that are still meaningful today, it is baffling how Fassbinder's textual and narrative constructs, and his notion of a non-identitarian subject, are in full accordance with post-structuralist abstractions. This conceptual framework did not result from any theoretical endeavor, not following or illustrating any particular set of ideas. And although it overlaps with topics that could certainly have been discussed in academic contexts at the time, it was decades ahead of reviewers and cinephiles.

In my view, that is reason enough to discuss Fassbinder's *BA* in more vivid detail. It provides sufficient points of reference for a broad approach, for digressions, and to act as a filter for current phenomena. And what is said here about this miniseries will of course also apply to many of the director's other works.

My tacit assumption here is that movies are not usually considered capable of playing any real part in major intellectual currents, let alone anticipating them. I make this assumption in spite of the huge increase in academic discourse on film over recent decades. This upsurge of intimidating and intimidated discourse has also led to a certain smugness of the "theoretical," and the use of names, concepts, and theorems as mere ornaments, resulting in a devaluation of particularities or the films themselves. Often enough, they are abused as theoretical utilities and cited merely to bolster assertions of prejudice, topicality, or pop-cultural acumen. This in turn crushes any possibility of their acting as a vehicle or example by which to grasp the function of artistic production—this function having already been fulfilled by their ability to be exploited as an academic object.

In this case, however, the work is one of a kind. Does that make hermeneutics inevitable? Does the project risk being overly retrospective? Perhaps. (After all, we are talking about a thirty-four-year-old film adaptation of an eighty-five-year-old book, and the resulting theoretical concerns are also not especially novel.) I am prepared to dismiss such concerns, and I also cannot help asking another even more disreputable question: Which paths of thought did Fassbinder follow to arrive at his aesthetic conceptions? Today, it is customary for artists to offer their own rationalizations, declaring their inspirations, sources, and objectives as part and parcel of their work. Since this was not the case with Fassbinder, one must more or less rely on the evidence provided by his films. In general, it seems fair to assume a heuristic and intuitive dimension, a process largely uninhibited by external factors, constantly refining preferences and methods, constantly surpassing itself, based on constant production.

Although it might be interesting to explore this question in biographical terms,[6] it is far more easily answered from another angle. After all, most of what I have just described as the exceptional quality and striking topicality of Fassbinder's film was dictated by Alfred Döblin's 1929 novel—based on the specific structure of the original text, its levels of narrative, constellations of characters, plot elements, and specific management of complexity.

The primary artistic acts here, then, were the selection of material and the retelling of Döblin's narrative. On this basis, and through the given material, Fassbinder introduced conceptual

6 The question will remain unanswered. But my interest in Fassbinder's possible theoretical horizon was sufficient to prompt my sole excursion in the guise of biographer. Had he, for example, read Freud, the post-structuralists, etc.? Harry Baer, who worked for years as production researcher on *BA*, was unable to provide any information. In the sparsely furnished room where the director lived during the three-year production phase, Baer told me, the shelves contained far more gay porn videos than printed matter (interview, May 28, 2009). Another contact, his ex-wife and frequent collaborator, Ingrid Caven, was also unable to help (interview, July 21, 2009).

layers of his own. He added the act of reading as a productive force and, in so doing, gained access to a historical dimension. Fassbinder's reading of Döblin was like the reactivation of a disused subway line that connects the present with the past, but in reverse.[7] Döblin's novel was not given a revisionist update from the point of view of the present. The opposite is true: the novel provided a point of departure from which to historicize the German present—by regressing to earlier manifestations (which is what gives the film *BA* its specific weight).

This approach, taking on another author's literary text, also bypasses all the usual yardsticks for film adaptations (appropriateness, accomplishment, congeniality). At no point can the film version be separated from its source text or played off against it. Just as Döblin's epic was not intended as "literature" in the traditional sense, Fassbinder's epic is not a "film." This also casts doubt on its merits as a cinephile object. Not everything takes place within the same frame of reference. In spite of the considerable weight, force, and scope of *BA*, its center of gravity lies outside its mass as an audiovisual artifact.

The idea that this madness of over fifteen hours and fourteen parts was once shown at prime time on German public television, which at the time had just three channels, is perfectly astonishing. But in 1980, the message largely missed its mark—it was spoken into the wind.

7 I apologize for this rather strained image, which is borrowed from Emir Kusturica's *Underground* (1995). This film, too, presents Europe's history in the twentieth century as a panorama, focusing on former Yugoslavia. During or immediately after the Yugoslav wars, in the early 1990s, the main figures, who have fled to Germany, lift up a manhole cover in front of the Reichstag in Berlin. It is the entrance to an underground transportation network linking the capital cities of Europe. A non-historicizing but otherwise similar metaphor was used by Martin Kippenberger for his *Metro-Net* installations—a series of entrances to subway stations built at various locations around the globe.

The Themes Are (Not) There for the Taking

In 1930, Döblin's publisher S. Fischer promoted his book with the following words: "A harrowing human destiny—a breathtaking crime novel—a portrait of the underworld—a major event in contemporary literature—*Berlin Alexanderplatz*." In a way, this was more accurate, and less focused on characters, than most blurbs today. Fassbinder remarked that *BA* was "basically nothing more than a threepenny novel, nothing more than just a series of several tabloid features."[1] And Döblin himself said of the novel's protagonist, Franz Biberkopf: "He has realized that what matters is not being a so-called decent person, but finding the right *Nebenmenschen* [companions, fellow human beings]. This realization helps him to find himself again. By connecting with his new surroundings, he also rediscovers his self-assurance in life."[2]

Fassbinder's film version of *BA*, however, can and in fact must be described differently. Its topography is more adequately illustrated by taking a more freewheeling approach, sampling from across the series to look at individual thematic cells and lines of discourse.

1 Rainer Werner Fassbinder, "The Cities of Humanity and the Human Soul: Some Unorganized Thoughts on Alfred Döblin's Novel *Berlin Alexanderplatz*" (originally published in *Die Zeit*, March 14, 1980), in *The Anarchy of the Imagination: Interviews, Essays, Notes; Rainer Werner Fassbinder*, ed. Michael Töteberg and Leo A. Lensing, trans. Kristina Winston (Baltimore: John Hopkins University Press, 1992), 166.

2 Quoted from the cover of the first German edition.

Opening Sequence. The opening composition is in a category of its own. Over a selection of period photographs fading into one another, locomotive wheels spin, going nowhere under full steam. Looking back to the 1920s, these images establish a documentary frame prior to the dramatic fiction. They show the appearance of Berlin, summing up social and political realities around 1928, but they also document what the film itself will not reconstruct in this form: unemployed people, at the labor exchange, looking for work, demonstrating ("Extortionate Rents," "Strike!," "We Demand Work & Bread," "Down with the Finance Minister"), large crowds, lots of police, mainly to quell uprisings, then nightlife, cabarets and cinemas, pornographic photographs; homeless people, prisoners, food queues, war invalids; Alfred Döblin with a patient in his doctor's office, a bowl of food being passed through the hatch in the door of a prison cell.

Cities, Places. Features associated with the "city novel" dominate the reception of *BA* the novel, although Döblin evokes "the city" primarily by naming streets, bars, and shops. But this is enough to tell us that his Berlin consists solely of the impoverished Scheunenviertel and other neighborhoods around Alexanderplatz. There are streets with prostitutes, corner pubs, and thieves' hideouts, plus various municipal and state institutions (court, social security office, police station, insane asylum, Salvation Army, prison, slaughterhouse). [BERLIN SUPER-CITY] The special form Döblin gives to Berlin is not based on external empirical knowledge, consisting instead of an interweaving of class-specific forms of speech. To this is added a mythical dimension (Job, Whore of Babylon), reinforced by metaphors of the underground (subway, slaughterhouse, hell, insanity).

The panorama created by Döblin in this way is narrowed down in Fassbinder's work. Although the film's locations include streets, intermediate levels in subway stations, red-light districts, courtyards, and staircases, its key settings are "apartment" and "pub." While the former is a place of private terrors and joys, the latter is a social hub. This is where people go to escape the sadness of family life or solitude, or just to find out what's going on. In the pub, deliberate or unplanned exchanges can take place, even across lines of social hierarchy. By contrast, the apartments are prisonlike. In other films, too, Fassbinder created interiors that were particularly cramped, an effect heightened in *BA* by the presence of miniature forms (birdcage, aquarium). As such, they resemble the "enclosed milieus" of the institutional and public sphere—the prison, the insane asylum, and the slaughterhouse that are also featured in *BA*.

Economy, Work, Money, Social Stratification. BA mixes different registers and economies, but the material aspect (money and the conditions of its acquisition) remains the inescapable starting point. In the late 1920s, the economy was at rock bottom and joblessness had reached record levels. As a worker, Franz Biberkopf (played in the film by Günter Lamprecht) is thus utterly dispensable. (At one point, he goes into detail naming the current figures: in Berlin alone, 673,582 unemployed, 673,583 including himself.) Although Biberkopf must content himself with the lousiest of jobs, he is the only one in his social circle who still believes in something like the dignity of labor. In spite of this, the "proletarian" as a historical subject is pushed to the margins in *BA*; heavy physical or factory work barely figures. And the few who do have a regular job are hardly better off. The central class here is the subproletariat—living hand to mouth, from state subsidies, or scraping along by moonlighting or providing illegal services.

Otherwise, the social panorama in *BA* is based strictly on minorities. There are communists, rabbis and Jewish sausage salesmen, anarcho-syndicalists, Nazis and gay Nietzscheans, various prostitutes, criminals both petty and powerful, workers both unaffiliated and with party ties. The one thing we don't see is families or representatives of the middle or upper classes.

Crime, Prostitution. For Döblin/Fassbinder, the big-time capitalist and the big-time criminal were pivotal players in society, ruthless legislators of their own realpolitik. The criminal milieu is both a reflection and a parody of legal economic relations. Burglaries, too, are productions calling for the latest methods of management and distribution. The office of gang leader Pums (Ivan Desny) is thus one of the few interiors where Fassbinder's film does justice to the decorative arts of the 1920s.

The parody in *BA* is taken to the point that prostitutes and burglars become advocates of (petty) bourgeois conditions and thinking (debts must always be repaid, order is of paramount importance). One conspicuous example is Meck (Franz Buchrieser), a gang member and longstanding friend of Biberkopf's: "Trade keeps the trader's belly full" (*BA*/2); "You want to be able to afford something" (*BA*/5).[3] Plus his not infrequent attacks of resignation: "Hard luck for some, so that others get the breaks" (*BA*/7). Biberkopf objects to this, saying that it depends what one is prepared to relinquish in the name of money, security, and comfort.

But Biberkopf's moral standards are corruptible, though not so easily. In the middle of the series, he is pushed into a special kind of transaction by his new friend Reinhold (Gottfried John). As Reinhold quickly tires of his partners, but wishes to avoid the strain of separation, he surprises Biberkopf by proposing

3 Quotes from the television series are taken from the English subtitles on the Criterion Collection DVD edition, with some minor adjustments. The numbers after individual quotes refer to the episode from which they are taken; ellipses take the place of omitted dialogue.

that he take over his girlfriends from him. At first, Biberkopf turns down the offer. But in the end, as the deal has not only sexual but also material benefits, Reinhold persuades him. And his arguments are quite crude: winter is approaching and he reminds Franz: "She has no real winter clothes, only autumn things—that could turn out to be expensive" (*BA*/5).

In less calculated ways, too, material concerns have a profound impact on relationships and feelings. For most of the characters, personal advantage—taking what one can get—is the strongest motivation for social interaction.

The most openly economized form of interpersonal relations is prostitution. Here, it is a stand-in for other deformations of thinking and feeling that are both required and produced by capitalist economic activity.

Marriage is based on a logic similar to that governing prostitution, but is considered more valuable on account of its legally binding nature and its higher price. In *BA*, however, the role played by marriage is negligible.

Welfare State. An important element of institutionalized social intercourse is the system of public social services. Alongside the police and the law, this system is the individual's most obvious experience of state intervention. Although many in *BA* receive such benefits, the welfare state has few advocates among its cast of figures. As well as beer-fueled bigotry, more advanced positions are also heard. In *BA*/7, a boastful dandy, the homosexual Willy (Fritz Schediwy), gives Biberkopf a piece of his Nietzschean mind, in spite of his own dependence on welfare payments: "The stupid thing in Germany is that they pay benefits. There are thousands running around, doing nothing, and getting paid for it."

Mass Communication. The city may regulate the "circulation of bodies," and capitalism may shape emotions, but the effects produced by mass media are more concrete. They fabricate discourses, put them into circulation, and supply thinking and "public opinion" with content that is hard to ignore. One only has to open a newspaper, switch on the radio, or watch a movie to connect with the distribution of a specific kind of knowledge. On the one hand, this means finding out all about murders, family tragedies, the life of celebrities, technical developments, sporting achievements, and the way love and sex are meant to work. On the other hand, one becomes a target for everyday propaganda, incorporating its content into one's own ideas. (Newspaper headlines: "Workers' Government in Oslo Toppled! Stuttgart Six-Day Cycling Race Over!"; "Child Abuse Scandal. Czech Jew Abducted Twenty Boys. Still No Arrest!") The very same themes are still in circulation today, in identical or similar form (two-tier healthcare, cuts to wages and benefits, freedom to take responsibility, protection of private property, social democracy as a pillar of the state). Unlike today, however, some public statements at the time had an openly antiparliamentarian stance. The prevailing tone is an aggressively militaristic nationalism characterized by a broad-brush approach and a lachrymose licking of wounds (a nation "stabbed in the back" by proletarian revolution, the "unlawful" Treaty of Versailles). An intertitle sums up this tendency: "The German Reich is a republic, and anyone who doesn't believe it will be shot in the neck" (*BA*/9). This aggressiveness is conveyed in the tone of public speakers, whose yelling, bleating, and bawling anticipate the style of Nazi orators. (Other such harbingers are also highlighted by Fassbinder: over the course of the series, Meck gradually trims the hair on his upper lip into what would soon be known only as the "Hitler moustache.")

Emotions, "Culture Industry." The media do not speak with a single voice, however. They can also show a friendly, comforting side, playing on "romantic" notions and longings. This is crucial to the impact achieved by the mass media. Popular songs (Richard Tauber, Irving Berlin) and sentimental newspaper stories may exploit emotions—but they can also express them, by telling the truth as a lie, so to speak. (An intertitle in *BA*/10: "Both know it's just a market song, where the music drones on; but still they have to weep when it's over, for sometimes life's too short for undying emotions.")

Political Alternatives, The Proletarian as Historical Subject. Alongside the production of opinions and ideas by mass media, there is also a focus on the materials and themes communicated by organizations and political parties (communism, anarcho-syndicalism, Nazis, Salvation Army). Biberkopf finds himself on various stages of fundamental political opposition, adapting to the discourses and concepts on offer in each case. He is in favor of order and a strong state, at the same time as being against all forms of oppression. He identifies weak points in arguments and political positions (fetishization of labor, the anarchist fiction of the general strike as a key instrument in the "proletarian struggle"). Although there are many references to fields of left-wing politics, including many positive ones, both Döblin and Fassbinder were skeptical. In public statements, Döblin repeatedly chafed at the orthodoxies, parties, and hero worship of the Left, as well as its penchant for "revolutionary boyscouting."

Although Biberkopf himself is unsuited to the role of "proletarian hero," as he almost never works, he does occasionally come into contact with such individuals. In *BA*/10 he listens to the lengthy lament of a worker about his ailing wife, exploitative employers, and the class bias in the education and healthcare systems: "I don't need Marx to understand when I'm being ripped off. But it's true nevertheless."

In many cases, however, there is no such direct contact. At one point, in *BA*/4, a drunken Biberkopf harangues a coal deliverer who carries on working impassively, untouched by the other man's delirious insights. ("We swore it to Karl Liebknecht. We stretch out our hands to Rosa Luxemburg. I'll go to paradise when I die, and they'll bow down before me and say, 'That's Franz Biberkopf, loyal and true, a German; does odd jobs, loyal and true. High flies the banner, black, white, and red, but he kept it to himself. He didn't turn to crime, like the others who want to be Germans, and who cheat their fellow citizens.'") Slightly later, watching a group of road workers, a similar outpouring: "Well, we can do that as well. Later. You hold it with your right hand, pull it up, hold it tight, then down it comes! Bang! That's working people for you! That's us, the proletariat. Up the right! Down the left! Bang! Up the right! Down the left. Bang!"

Education, Learning and Thinking. Although attempts at thinking for oneself may lead to contradictions or speculative dead ends, life is nonetheless a never-ending process of thinking and learning. After his first, moderate traumatization in *BA*/3, Biberkopf remarks, "If I had learned that, I'd have learned a lot more as well"; "I've learned something that I never wanted to learn." His education continues in this vein. In *BA*/8 he says, "I had a lot to learn about life and so on." And in *BA*/13: "If he doesn't learn, he'll never know anything. You run around like an idiot with no knowledge of the world."

If you want to learn, you have to be open to new ideas and ways of thinking. In this regard, Biberkopf is taken in hand by the opinionated Willy: "You understand? Nietzsche. Anything else is drivel, old boy" (*BA*/10); "Thinking is one of the very few things in the world that doesn't cost anything" (*BA*/9).

Out of pragmatism, the petit-bourgeois subject is drawn in the opposite direction. In the view of Frau Bast (Brigitte Mira), the friendly landlady, "There's no sense in brooding, especially if it doesn't help" (*BA*/3). And the prostitute Eva (Hanna Schygulla) is against anything that could disrupt public order, including Biberkopf's interest in political alternatives.

Anyone who does try to think, however, may soon find themselves in a state of confusion, like Biberkopf: "That it's possible to talk and think for and against the same thing at the same time. It's really strange" (*BA*/9).

Good Life, Needs, Demands. The need to learn and to think about the world may be driven by the desire for more satisfactory interpersonal relations, for freedom and a better world. This desire also shapes personal demands. People want to eat well, have plenty to drink, wear nice clothes, enjoy themselves, and find a sympathetic partner. These demands, too, are the subject of official discourse, but they cannot be satisfied by it. Ultimately, people themselves know best what is good for them and what they need. Biberkopf: "People should be free"; "People should decide for themselves what is good for them"; "What people need is what they need, simple as that."

Arrogance. Thinking necessarily leads to contradiction; emotions are "conservative," but they are also an invaluable path to knowledge. Biberkopf seldom walks this path, however. Armor-plating the ego is the central theme of *BA*, a theme explored in many variations. This insistence on a position of personal autonomy is reinforced by the historical context of the period following World War I, where extreme militarism and widespread political militancy provide a template and a point of reference for personal delusions of grandeur. Biberkopf: "I have my fists." He also has an undying love of soldier songs. Such examples of male empowerment are not the exception. At one point, Meck issues a threat: "I have a knife in my pocket. I always have a knife in my pocket" (*BA*/3).

At the same time, as another symptom of the postwar crisis, the myth of Germany having been "stabbed in the back" was painted as a collective castration. The economic crisis may have rendered finding a legal occupation almost impossible, but the ideal of self-reliance remains intact. (Biberkopf in *BA*/9: "What I need, I do myself. I'm self-sufficient.")

Masculinity. In spite of this, the position of the male is in decline in *BA*. Masculinity is widely experienced as unstable, and clues to Biberkopf's disturbed gender identity are given from the outset. Following his release from jail, he visits a prostitute, but he is unable to perform. Only when he rapes Minna (Karin Baal), the sister of his manslaughter victim Ida (Barbara Valentin), is his sexual function reestablished. In *BA*/4, when he spurns the advances of a good-looking neighbor, she hisses "limp dick" at him as she leaves. But Biberkopf knows that although he's not the sharpest knife in the drawer, he's always been good enough in bed.

In *BA*, "manliness" is forever being discussed, tested, or called into question. At a dance hall in *BA*/2, there is a test-your-strength machine ("For 20 pfennig you can find out if you're a man"). Here, Biberkopf meets the requirements. Minutes later, at the bar, the sales manager of the Nazi-affiliated *Völkischer Beobachter* newspaper puts the question slightly differently: "Are you a German man? Hmm? German to the core?" This time, Biberkopf merely shrugs his shoulders.

Incidental stories complete the picture. One such story involves the deterioration that comes with age: an acquaintance tells Biberkopf how the onset of rheumatism was followed by the removal of first one testicle (*BA*/4) and then the second.

Even in the criminal milieu, otherwise portrayed classically enough as a sphere where destructive and selfish impulses prevail, successfully realized male roles are thin on the ground. The members of the Pums gang may be many things—resilient, melancholic, nice, tearful, slimy, devious, shy, or brooding—but one thing they are not is "proper" men. No one here conforms to the "strong, silent type" so longed for in later times by Tony Soprano. (Fassbinder repeatedly addressed the crisis of the male role in his other films. In *In a Year of 13 Moons* from 1978, the transsexual protagonist Elvira defines "the masculine" as follows: "active, decisive, independent-seeming." In his production of Carlo Goldoni's *The Coffee Shop*, one character says, "What makes a man a man is that he can decide freely." But Fassbinder also liked to use exaggerated forms of masculinity: men in suits and fedoras who treat women badly "because that's the way they need it," like Raúl Gimenez as a Latin-lover terrorist in *The Third Generation*.)

Reinhold, too, for all his devilish attributes, is affected by the crisis of masculinity. In *BA*/5, his ex-girlfriend Cilly (Annemarie Düringer) says of him: "Reinhold's not a man … he's a sparrow … peck, peck." (This knowledge will not keep her from going back to him and coolly, calmly watching as he ditches another woman just as she was ditched before.)

But it is Biberkopf who is most seriously affected by these problems. The loss of his right arm is the most direct and drastic metaphor for this, reinforcing doubts that were already there before. The narrator says: "We have legs, we have teeth, we have eyes, we have arms. Just let someone come and try to bite us or bite Franz! Just let someone come. He's got two arms, two legs; he's got muscles. He'll beat everything to a pulp. Just let someone get to know Franz! He's no pushover. What we've been through, what we still have to go through. Just let someone emulate that! We'll drink to it, two drinks, nine drinks."

Biberkopf answers: "We have no legs, we have no teeth, we have no eyes, we have no arms. Anyone can come along and bite Franz. He's a pushover. He can't defend himself. All he can do is drink" (*BA*/13).

In spite of such outbreaks of self-pity, the man in Biberkopf is constantly rebelling. The self-interest and illusions of the ego prove persistent, repeatedly prompting him to bouts of boasting and life-and-death struggles for recognition.

Narcissism, Self-Preservation. Döblin associates his critique of the male position with the fight against narcissism. Baumann (Gerhard Zwerenz): "Did you lose your heart to nature?" Biberkopf: "I didn't lose my heart there." Baumann: "Did you lose your heart to sports? In the roar of the youth movement? In the turmoil of politics?" Biberkopf: "I didn't lose it there." Baumann: "So you haven't lost it anywhere? Are you the type of person who doesn't lose his heart anywhere, but keeps it for himself, conserves it clinically, mummifies it?" (*BA*/4). It is Biberkopf's insistence on personal autonomy and a distinct identity that must be destroyed or relinquished. The narrative model for this destruction is the story of Job.

Homosexuality. As one of the strongest markers of shifting gender lines in *BA*, homosexuality lies deep in the folds of this scenario of manliness under fire. Even the media industry has identified a new demand and has begun to produce educational literature for various target groups (initially for sale under the counter), thus pursuing "identity politics" via pornographic means. Biberkopf: "Aha ... *Love Between Women.* All available separately" (*BA*/2). As he is considering going into this line of business himself, he takes a pile of magazines to examine at home. One article in particular arouses his pity. It tells of a homosexual love affair that ends up in court as a case of blackmail, destroying the lives of those involved. Biberkopf thinks this is unjust, and his girlfriend Lina (Elisabeth Trissenaar) now thinks he's gay.

Many first encounters between men are staged by Fassbinder as sexual advances. Attentive looks are exchanged, their meaning only becoming clear seconds later. This happens with the sales director of the *Völkischer Beobachter* and with a paperboy in *BA*/10, who reacts very aggressively to Biberkopf's gaze ("What's up? Why are you staring like that?").

In *BA*/7, Biberkopf also meets a genuine homosexual. Willy is a dandy with a vicious tongue who bad-mouths "cripples" and social-welfare benefits. His scorn thus extends to the amputee Biberkopf, who replies, "You know, you're only ten to twelve years younger than we are, but you're a hundred years smarter. Boy, if I'd dared talk like that when I was twenty, it would have been: 'Hands out of your pockets and stand up straight!'" To which Willy cheerfully replies, "It's the same with us, only not out of our own pockets," and kisses his boyfriend on the cheek. This boyfriend, played by Udo Kier, represents a different type of homosexual: simple-minded, amiable, unambitious, slow-witted.

In any case, Biberkopf is so taken with Willy that he seeks closer contact with him, in turn getting the other man's hopes up. During Willy's first visit, Biberkopf beats around the bush like someone about to come out. But then he says what he really wants from the other man—a part in his business of dealing in stolen goods. (As he leaves, Willy smells a blue flower and inspects the nails of his splayed fingers.) The two of them become friends nonetheless, and Willy initiates Biberkopf into the world of ideas and "politics." This is not to Eva's liking: "He's leading Franz astray." She is referring to the "political" milieu of the losers, layabouts, and have-nots, and she almost jealously encourages Biberkopf's lover Mieze (Barbara Sukowa) to keep him as far from this man as possible (*BA*/10).

It may seem, then, that Fassbinder gave *BA* an overly "homosexualized" reading, and he himself was also sometimes under this impression. In fact, he differs from Döblin in just one respect: Fassbinder was working as an openly gay man, whereas Döblin was a husband and father. (In spite of this, many of his texts display a marked interest in the beefiness of big strong men. His other novels, too, contain homoerotic scenes, some of them quite bawdy.)

Finally, Fassbinder's "homosexualizations" are entirely justified by the novel, where corresponding signs are generously spread throughout. But Fassbinder did make additions on the level of bit parts and in the background of scenes. He also agreed with Döblin on one crucial point: Fassbinder, too, did not assume that "everything is available separately." Neither version of *BA* affirms a conception of homosexuality as identity or minority.

At any rate, *BA* does not show concrete acts or explicit portrayals (apart from a prison scene with Reinhold and Konrad in *BA*/14). Homosexuality figures here within the expanded framework of ambivalent ties between men. Which is why their business is so often conducted in that most inviolable bastion of gender segregation, the gentlemen's toilets. And why women are so often the currency that establishes ties between men and keeps their exchanges in motion.

Even Willy sleeps with women, and Reinhold, who consumes them in such great numbers, is actually disgusted by them ("There are too many broads around anyway"; *BA*/5). Such relations between men conducted through women take concrete form in the abovementioned rotation scheme initiated by Reinhold. As he says to Mieze in *BA*/11: "You don't think I want to steal him, do you? I can resist that. But there were some strange things between him and me. … He really didn't tell you about them? … We used to swap broads, Franz and me."

Later in the same episode comes a slightly different bedroom scene. Biberkopf wants to reform Reinhold's attitude toward women, wants him to see for himself how satisfying an enduring relationship can be. To facilitate this, he hides Reinhold in his bed. But the presentation of the idyll goes wrong; Biberkopf goes berserk and gives Mieze a brutal beating. When Reinhold comes to her aid, she utters piercing screams of despair, immediately realizing her role as the powerless party in a dreadful triangle. (Later she tells Eva: "He was lying in bed there, hidden under the covers. … It's funny, isn't it?" Eva: "No, I don't think it's funny. There's something behind it, Mieze, something bad. … He hides him in his bed—and something like this happens.")

The high point and clearest indication of this convoluted structure is given in an intertitle: "And while he's dancing with Eva, inwardly he loves two people: One is his Mieze, whom he wishes could be there. The other is … Reinhold."

Women. This structure is supported and maintained by men alone. Looked at this way, *BA* is a "men's film." Women are mere objects, though indispensable as such. This could be used to underpin the accusations of misogyny that have often been leveled against Fassbinder. Such claims may or may not be valid. In an interview from 1980, when asked what was different about women in comparison to men, he answered, "Nothing at all."[4] And in *BA* there is not only violence against women, but also against men, although this admittedly takes place on a different level.

Below the level of this key constellation, however, Fassbinder created an extraordinarily rich inventory of female characters, "types," and "subjectivities." They include: Lina (worldly-wise, clairvoyant, courageous, sentimental, a woman with spirit and

4 Fassbinder, interview by Limmer/Rumler (1980), in Fischer, *Fassbinder über Fassbinder*, 530.

initiative), Fränze (Helen Vita, thick-skinned, affectionate, good-natured, with an "elastic heart"), Cilly (alluring, fashionable, can be cutting and condescending, but also very understanding), Trude (Irm Hermann, meek, mouselike, devoted, but insistent in her devotion: "Please, please don't hurt me—I love you").

Biberkopf's landlady Frau Bast is a representative of old-fashioned homeliness and of considerate, "boringly conventional" German people with no ulterior motives. She can always be depended on to provide a cup of "good," "freshly brewed" coffee. She may adopt the abrasive posture of a mother-in-law, but she is also easily won over and then she helps in whatever way she can. As the woman on the threshold, Frau Bast is a constant witness to the events, both happy and monstrous, that unfold in the rooms she rents out.

As an ingenue, Mieze is an exceptional figure in Fassbinder's oeuvre: totally open, impulsive, "loves everyone and everything,"[5] incapable of jealousy. She is the opposite of the hysterical woman with masochistic and passive-aggressive tendencies to whom Fassbinder erected so many great monuments. Sexually, as a prostitute, she is not focused on a single person, and in every other way, too, she is open to unusual relationships and forms of cohabitation. She pushes Biberkopf into pimping her. She refuses to use the "feminine tricks" recommended to her by Eva, at one point falling in love with another man, which has no effect on her feelings for Biberkopf ("I'm yours"). He finds it less easy to relinquish his claim to exclusivity.

But there are also brief moments of solidarity between women. After being beaten up by Biberkopf in *BA*/11, Mieze arrives at an out-of-town restaurant looking very much the worse for wear; a concerned waitress mumbles to herself, "What have they done to you?"

5 Ibid., 518.

Another form of solidarity occurs in an unexpected place: to an almost provocative degree, most of the actors in *BA* are too old, compared both with the descriptions in Döblin's novel and with prevailing film conventions. Helen Vita and Annemarie Düringer were over fifty at the time (as was Günter Lamprecht, whereas Fassbinder was in his mid-thirties). This means that many of the female figures here are basically unattractive, not only by today's standards. In spite of this, they play sexually desirable characters without their age being an issue or their erotic credibility being compromised (this, too, is an aspect of "play," make-believe, and fictionality).

Sympathy, Kindness, Care. Well-meaning affection is not an exclusively female quality in *BA*, although it is seen with above-average frequency in female characters. Caring, considerate, and gentle contact also exists between men. This is especially true of the older men, the kindly publican (who gives his guests psychological and legal advice) or Baumann, who accompanies Biberkopf's crisis-ridden transition to a new phase of life in *BA*/4 with great forbearance as the incarnation of death (lets him do as he pleases, plays games with him, clears up his vomit, shares the last bottle of beer with him).

Cynicism. Such constructive emotions are thin on the ground, however, and positive approaches are constantly threatened by antagonistic behavior. An important subcategory of this depravity is cynicism, especially in the form embodied by Reinhold. With his partly superhuman qualities, he, too, is an exceptional figure. He "has the power of almighty God," as well as attributes of the devil (he is unscrupulous, brutal but seductive, quick-tempered, awkward, with a stutter). Reinhold wants to draw Biberkopf into the world of crime. At the same time, he displays an almost infantile narcissism. He is dominated by feelings of pleasure and unpleasure; aversion and disgust are his most common emotions. He has no capacity for good deeds. On the contrary, irritable as he is, he always wants to immediately be rid of whatever gets on his nerves.

Collectivity. BA poses the question of what binds people together, of how collectivities are formed and maintained. These may be friendships, sexual relationships, groups, or gangs. The key question is whether and how one has learned to lift oneself out of indifference and put one's energies and abilities to uses beyond self-interest. One is never entirely self-created, always depending on *Nebenmenschen*. Functioning bonds are also found in the shadows of prostitution. The main element here is *philia*: not begrudging the other person what she has, what she deserves, and what is good for her.

Talking, Giving. Talk is the strongest binding link between people in *BA*. But this relies on the other person being gripped by it, which may also occur through small talk or banter. But such a connection is hindered by the airing of opinions and the use of functionalized speech. The various effects of speech are addressed directly in *BA*. Mieze to Biberkopf: "Talk to me. It's not fair." Then later, to Reinhold: "You can talk straight with me. Do you understand?" (*BA*/12).

This form of speech that grips the addressee establishes a link to narrative. For Döblin, the functions of storytelling included "therapy" and self-help. Biberkopf goes through many "talking cures," although their effect is not necessarily a lasting one. He will never manage to lose a certain "German" character ("Attention! Keep going forward … left right left right. … No use pretending you're tired," he says in *BA*/9—outside a brothel).

In affairs of the heart, things are different again. Unlike friendships, relationships based on love require both sides to accept dependence and negotiate terms of ownership. Mieze is the most spectacular case of willingly and unconditionally becoming property. In *BA*/11, she tells Biberkopf, "I'm yours, Franz. I belong to you, you alone." Biberkopf has a similar view, but his answers on this point remain contradictory. He wants friendship and love, but he also insists on his boundaries and autonomy. Concerning Reinhold, an interesting reversal takes place: "Hands off him, Herbert! He's not yours. He belongs to me. To me" (*BA*/13).

The forces that aim to create bonds are disturbed by the antagonistic forces of greed, scheming, selfishness, and self-interest—by means including forms of speech that are abusive and manipulative or that create distance. Again and again, Biberkopf is held back by childish claims. He often rejects offers of help ("I'll help myself"). After his amputation, he can no longer afford the same degree of stubbornness. The loss of his arm turns him back into the needy child that he himself claims to always have remained. But now he must actively ask for help, submitting to Mieze's maternal regime without complaint. He lets her wash him like a baby, even between his legs (*BA*/12).

Prostitution, Pornography. Institutionalized forms of relieving libidinal tension are a major disruptive factor in human relations. Prostitution and pornography cater to sexual needs at the point where they are most easily aroused and satisfied—they alienate the erotic into commodity form. Biberkopf knows: "It starts with looking at pictures; and later, when you want to, it doesn't come natural anymore" (*BA*/2).

Storytelling, too, can go both ways. In *BA*/9, the bouncer in the red-light district regales Franz with a story. Biberkopf thinks it's "hot" and proceeds to tell one of his own that's not so hot. The other man doesn't rate it, but he consoles Biberkopf: "That's something you can learn: how to tell stories."

Hysterics, Neurotics. It is fitting to comment here on Fassbinder's system of characters. The cast of all of his films can be divided roughly into two groups: figures of passage and figures of blockade. The former tend to be hysterics, the latter neurotics. The neurotics are at one with their (petit) bourgeois values, have precise notions of what is appropriate and what is unacceptable. They are anxious, opportunist, shrewd, often supercilious, caustic, fretful, opinionated, and socially aspiring. They terrorize those around them with meanness, contempt, bitterness, and malicious gossip. The neurotics appear as neighbors, shop owners, or family members, and as evil or calculating mothers. They can be officials, salesmen, and accountants. They are responsible for many disruptions of the social and are utterly unsuited to interaction based on love and friendship. They are also distributed across borders of age, gender, and class. (Fassbinder, who usually resisted clear typecasting, found in Hark Bohm an actor who embodied the petit-bourgeois grumbler with a rare astringency. In *BA* he plays Lüders, who triggers Biberkopf's first trauma. And even in the hellish world of *BA*/14, he recites the whiny credo of petit-bourgeois self-pity; asked by Biberkopf how he is, he replies, "Not well at all, actually.")

Exceptions from this pattern are figures of what might be called semi-passage, in particular a certain type of "modern" women: lively, assertive, hardly restricted by conventions, keen to use opportunities, and thus suited to pursuing a career. A staple of Fassbinder's films, such characters are played more often than not by Hanna Schygulla, sometimes also by Ingrid Caven. As Lili, Maria, Veronika, or Lola, they occupy central positions in his later "history" films about Germany.

In *BA*, this semi-passage type is represented by Eva. Here, too, her character traits are contradictory: pragmatic, shrewd, politically conservative, comradely, and generous. She tries repeatedly to help Biberkopf, including offers of financial assistance. As his former lover, she has never fully separated from him; she makes sexual advances to him several times, but she also introduces him to Mieze. Eva is critically defined via her relationship with her own body: appreciates fine fabrics, focuses on personal hygiene, articulates sexual demands, engages in autoeroticism—in front of mirrors.

Men with similarly "modern" traits are rare in Fassbinder's work. But he did create a number of striking upper-middle-class characters in their older years. Experience has made them serene, worldly-wise, and understanding. As such, they also represent a degree of maturity that has overcome narcissism. In *BA*, such characters are played by Ivan Desny as Pums and Adrian Hoven as Mieze's regular john.

The figures clearly preferred by Fassbinder, however, are the hysterics, to whom he devotes a large part of his thinking and his artistic attention. Although not present in large numbers, they often appear as central characters in his films. The reason for this preference is that only through them and in them can something decisive take place. In the given social contexts, they are unwilling or unable to function. This disaccord manifests itself not as a "critique" but in a suffering they have learned to bear or enjoy.

Although the hysterics in Fassbinder's films are mostly women, he makes no gender-specific limitations. In *BA*, the hysteric is a man, Biberkopf himself. As such he complements Erwin/Elvira from *In a Year of 13 Moons.*

Freeform Families, Social Costs. The social panorama outlined here leaves little room for utopian demands. In fact, Fassbinder almost never clearly formulated what he wished for in societal or political terms. But he did admit (or signal a wish) that successful forms of coexistence were possible, even if only on the small scale of what might be called freeform families, though not within the framework of state, party, or nuclear family.

While families as long-term legal entities were subjected to scrutiny in many of Fassbinder's films, they play no part in *BA*. His films rarely feature children, and, significantly, never babies or infants.[6]

In *BA*, he installed an ersatz mother in the form of Frau Bast, which has no basis in the novel. Elsewhere, too, he "familialized" the original: at one point, Biberkopf asks Meck, "Just one more question. I wanted to know if you ever had a father."

The film even includes an attempt at reproduction. Mieze wants a child from Biberkopf, and since she is unable to have one she asks Eva to step in as surrogate mother. This would be a practicable solution, as Eva's regular john wants a child from her and her boyfriend also has no objections to the arrangement. The child would have two prostitutes for mothers, and three fathers who are pimps and johns (the pregnancy ends in a miscarriage).

In *BA*/13, in another remarkable addition to the original, some members of the Pums gang wish to impose a more democratic model. Above all, they want to switch from stealing goods to stealing cash: "Money can be divided up precisely." On the other hand: "Goods are simply not as dangerous as

6 This is significant for the following reason: for the last two decades, in both film and literature, common sense and a universally valid perspective have been closely associated with family, genealogy, and reproduction—to the point of total inescapability. In films, this can be treated as a mere gimmick of dramaturgical expediency (threat/protection, care/responsibility) or as something to be taken for granted. Into the 1970s, the family as "terror cell" or "horror show" was a common-enough topos. Not only is this no longer possible, it is now almost inconceivable. Fundamental criticism has been replaced by the adjective "dysfunctional." Synonymous with "minor, potentially resolvable disorder," it forms the outermost limit of criticism. But this inescapability of the family is also one of the clearest signs of an erosion of the "political" in artistic fields. [German Calamities (1980–2010)]

money." The two sides in the dispute eye each other warily; there is talk of a vote. (Pums: "Take a vote? Ha! I haven't heard such baloney in a long time.") Adding to his argument in favor of cash, Meck adds: "What Reinhold says is true. Why should we all work for one guy? On the other hand, in my opinion, a genuine collaboration would be the finest thing of all."

Utopia, Pessimism. Fassbinder's oeuvre offers no example of a life well lived or the successful reconciliation of desires with reality (with the possible exception of the TV series *Eight Hours Are Not a Day*, since he believed the medium of television demanded a particular optimism).[7] In *BA*, multiple friendships are betrayed, love affairs often come to an abrupt and even brutal end.

Fassbinder's central article of faith comes to bear here, one on which he based the only utopian proposal he ever made: those who love are always in an inferior position to those who are loved. They are exploited, they always have to pay extra, because "love has a price," or, as Fassbinder often put it, "those who love forfeit their rights." Forfeiting rights, paying a high price—on this basis, suffering becomes a means of insight with emancipatory force. Although this force is obstructed by its strongest opponent: self-love.

Alternative Economies, Transgressions. Beyond the sphere of "bourgeois" and narcissistic interests, there lurks a fundamentally different order. Here, exchanges are not subject to negotiation, nor to one's own best judgment. Education, a belief in progress

7 Fassbinder: "I think that for television, you have to make films that are more relevant, more socially relevant than for the cinema. In the cinema, you can do more with dreams, work more as a dream factory. The television audience expects a certain degree of realism." Interview by Corinna Brocher (1972), in Fischer, *Fassbinder über Fassbinder*, 253.

and self-improvement, "knowledge is power," "emergence from self-imposed immaturity"—all this has no resonance in *BA,* coming up against its limits in the form of "the sacred" and the unconscious.

Biberkopf has several points of access to this sphere: dreams, traumas, fits of madness, and bouts of drinking. The effects of alcohol are varied: the drinker's brain and tongue are loosened, he becomes foolish and playful, feels stronger, mixes more easily with strangers. For Biberkopf, there are few things that cannot be resolved by alcohol, which is why he cannot get enough of it ("another schnapps"). It also helps him to stifle the painful and the unbearable. If he goes too far, he alienates himself from his surroundings, but sometimes also achieves moments of great clarity (*BA*/4).

Animal. To this end, the central authority of the brain must be evaded, or its functions must be expanded to include acephalous forms of perception and insight. Humans also think with their knees, arms, tongues, and guts—making them part of the animal world. Biberkopf knows that an animal, too, is a fellow creature endowed with feelings. An intertitle in *BA*/4 declares: "Man's fate is like that of the beasts: just as they die, so does he." While Biberkopf worries about the health of a bird vegetating in the smoky environment of his regular bar, he is also a carnivore of gargantuan proportions (his favorite dish is pig's ear with peas).

At the end of *BA*, Biberkopf wants to become an animal himself. He abjures speech and the upright gait. A comment from the narrator in *BA*/11 adds the following image: "The worms always eat dirt."

Victim, Trauma, Mental Block. For Biberkopf, however, eating meat is also associated with sacrifice and death (as inflicted millions of times every day on an industrial basis in the slaughterhouses).

But it is not only his great appetite that connects him with this sphere. In the prehistory of *BA*, he dealt some brutal blows, and now he must absorb some himself. His second traumatic experience, the loss of his right arm, takes on the character of a sacrifice. (It is also his first encounter with death.) In spite of this, Biberkopf never wastes much time complaining, accepting the amputation instead as given and necessary: "It's quite OK that the arm's gone. The arm had to go" (*BA*/7).

He thus acknowledges something that is hard to digest: all resources must be spent, all damage to one's own body must be accepted. What must be offloaded or sacrificed is cast off in the name of a higher good. This good might be called destiny (that is what Walter Benjamin called it in his review of *BA*: "He is consumed by a hunger for destiny").[8] Here, too, the rule applies: nothing comes for free, everything has its price—in fact, it must cost something, otherwise death takes place in life (which also introduces a drastic counterpart to the neoliberal contractual fiction of a win-win situation).

Biberkopf repeatedly suffers catatonic fits, the most severe in response to being told that his girlfriend has been murdered. Referred to a psychiatric profession that is rooted in nineteenth-century concepts and hardened by wartime abuses (electroshock), he is treated as a fake. A younger generation of doctors, more open to psychoanalytical methods, has yet to make an impact. (The senior physician in *BA*/14: "Maybe the autopsy will bring us a big surprise.")

Death. That life is a path to death is played out in many variations in *BA*. Early on, in *BA*/2, it is couched in economic terms

8 Walter Benjamin, "Crisis of the Novel: On Döblin's *Berlin Alexanderplatz*," (1930) in *Selected Writings*, ed. Michael W. Jennings, Howard Eiland, and Gary Smith, trans.

("How is one to live if one doesn't want to die?"). But then the theme of sacrifice comes to the fore (slaughterhouse, the ritual killing of a sheep, the story of Abraham and Isaac).

Whatever Biberkopf does, he is always confronted with the issue of death, even when buying flowers. (In *BA*/3: "They have to mean: the past keeps following you, driving you on and on, driving you somewhere where there's no future. … Do you understand?" "Yes, I understand you. What you need are carnations, white carnations, sir." "White carnations? But they're flowers for death, aren't they?")

Biberkopf's various retreats into solitude resemble deaths, and in *BA*/7 he realizes this himself: "I'm close to death. I feel it. About to kick the bucket." In the penultimate episode, an intertitle draws the starkest line under his life: "Franz Biberkopf has reached the end of his mortal path. The time has come to break him. The man is finished."

By this point, events have long since entered a very basic phase where life and death coexist "harmoniously" and form a cycle where life includes its future as goo. In a lament for Mieze, the voice-over says: "Her face is destroyed, her teeth are destroyed, her eyes are destroyed, her mouth, lips, tongue, and throat, her body, her legs, her womb. I am yours. You should comfort me. I'm not feeling well. Come on. We're nearly home. I am yours" (*BA*/13).

The narrator chimes in with Ecclesiastes 3:1: "To every thing there is a season … a time to be born, and a time to die; a time to plant and to pluck what is planted … a time to kill and to heal, to break down and build up; a time to keep, and a time to cast away; a time to rend and to sew; a time to keep silence, and to speak" (*BA*/12).

Rodney Livingstone et al., vol. 2, part 1, *1927–1930* (Cambridge, MA: Belknap Press of Harvard University Press, 1999), 303.

Paternal Authority, Desire. In *BA*, the social takes shape as a freeform family structure, economic activity takes place under the auspices of illegality, masculinity is fundamentally called into question. But the positions vacated on one level are reoccupied all the more forcefully on another—with an abstract fount of meaning, the severe God of the Old Testament. Always ready to inflict violent conditions and demand huge, incalculable sacrifices, he makes the same precautionary example of Biberkopf as he once did of Abraham and Job.

In *BA*, the Almighty is represented in negative form, so to speak, by Reinhold. And it is precisely Reinhold's violence that is the object of Biberkopf's desire. Initially, this leads to misjudgments and bitter disappointments, and to the last he says of Reinhold: "He's a good guy at heart." In the context of this narrative, however, disappointments and errors are necessary and inevitable, since desire, too, simultaneously deceives and does not deceive, and is capable of attaching itself to unsuitable objects and hostile, asymmetrical relationships. In *BA*, Döblin, in whose work (as in Fassbinder's) aporias tend to be writ large, gave these objects and relationships an especially tough and difficult edge. In this way, he was able to capture the logic of desire that casts the relationship between life instinct and death drive in contradictory, inescapable, near unbearable phenomena. In his desire for Reinhold, Biberkopf expresses his appetite for death.

Holocaust. Fassbinder in turn further heightened these drastic renderings. Into Döblin's sequence of revelations he inserted another, at whose virtual center stands the Holocaust. Although Döblin's novel predates this most extreme transgression in German history, he provided Fassbinder's reworking with motifs and points of reference with which to evoke this aspect (expressionist abjection, motif of the slaughterhouse and the morgue). A voice-over in *BA/4* states: “The importance of fats in nutrition. Fat acts as a covering for bone protuberances and protects the tissue beneath against pressure and impact. That’s why emaciated people complain of pains in their feet when they walk.”

Knowing what we do today, this chillingly clinical diagnosis inevitably appears to anticipate its “biopolitical” surpassing in Germany’s concentration camps.

Nuances of Modernity

> There is no very great merit in a rapid style and a casual mode of expression.
> —Marcel Proust

However precise one's descriptions, it is hard not to acknowledge that much of what can be said about Fassbinder's film also applies to Döblin's book. As well as giving the film its material, the book also determined its thinking and structure.

Unlike Fassbinder, however, Döblin always set out his aesthetic principles in candid and pithy terms. Many of these principles were based on negation. Regarding the literary output of his time, he focused on its defects and its compliance with convention: exaggeration of dramatic techniques and linear plots, narrative tricks and artful use of perspective, a fixation on psychology and bourgeois values in general (charges that could just as well be leveled at today's artistic productions). By contrast, he declared that "suspense ruins the novel," "the human individual is not the subject of drama or of the novel," "the novel has nothing to do with plot."[1] The novel has no need to entertain or teach, advocate theories, or feel tied to any rules, he argued. Instead, it can operate heterogeneously and without constraint. The author, meanwhile, need not be concerned with deliberate rule breaking or with flouting taboos of form

1 Alfred Döblin, "Bemerkungen zum Roman" [Remarks on the novel, 1917], in *Schriften zu Ästhetik, Poetik und Literatur*, ed. Erich Kleinschmidt (Olten: Walter, 1989), 124–25. This volume also includes the essays "Reform des Romans" [Reform of the novel, 1919], "Die Arbeit am Roman" [Work on the novel, 1928], and "Der Bau des epischen Werks" [Construction of the epic work, 1928], in which Döblin sets out his theory and praxis of the novel.

or content. A central concept for Döblin was that of *Dichtung* (poetic composition, literally "condensing," can also apply to literary prose). For him, *Dichtung* was everything that refrains from tricks and techniques and that constitutes narration itself instead of merely recounting a narrative. He referred to this type of writing as epic. For Döblin, the epic was synonymous with non-literature and anti-form—in positive terms, a sprawling approach to narrative facilitating insight in a range of ways based on disparate material drawn from reality.

Walter Benjamin took a similar, though more fundamental view. The modern novel, he claimed in his review of *BA,* is symptomatic of disorientation and crisis.[2] Specifically, he saw this reflected in the separation of storytelling from the oral tradition, a development he attributed to Flaubert's writerly novel and its adherents. In André Gide's *roman pur*, he saw literary production degraded to a playground of secondary realities where mute monologues are addressed to a reader conceived of as similarly silenced. Benjamin conceded that Döblin preserved the epic dimension, a verdict the novelist himself naturally shared. The two intellectuals had very similar ideas about the relationship between the written and the oral, literariness and direct address, fiction and fact. Except that Döblin was not so much interested in the exact course of the dividing line between them. His factographic aspirations even led him to slur these boundaries, by which he hoped to achieve an increase in immediacy, liveliness, and present-tenseness. Unlike the literarily inclined writer, the epic writer does not content himself with the treatment of literary problems, doesn't focus on writerly routine or producing an "oeuvre," and is opposed to secondary elaborations. Instead, he tries to dismantle safeguards and avoid the aestheticization and reification of meaning that are the perils of penman-

2 Benjamin, "Crisis of the Novel," 299–304.

ship. The epic writer should avoid easy beauty, but neither should he glorify ugliness and deliberate deformity.[3] He must guarantee the greatest possible input of reality in his work (an aim obstructed by literature as an institution and as an art form).

For Döblin, the epic was not specific to literature; it crossed media borders and did not even necessarily depend on the written form. Although he did not reject the novel out of hand—considering it potentially suited to a factographic project—it became conceivable, vital even, for the novel to converge with other media. Epic storytelling was to detach itself from the written word, or at least from its material (and culturally tainted) support, the book: "For a long time, my motto has been: Away from the book! But I see no clear path for today's epic writer, unless it is the path toward—a new stage."[4] Döblin did not say whether this new stage would be theater, radio, film, or some as yet unknown format. What counted was language, the flow of telling a story, which should ideally be open-ended[5]—as well as maximizing the direct inclusion of a wide range of factual material, coupled with a knowledge of society's workings and the way people actually speak in every social sphere. With these voices, Döblin thought, the epic writer draws the reader himself into the novel, thus raising the "iron curtain" between reader and author.

3 Responding to a survey in the *Berliner Börsen-Courier* from December 24, 1927, he said, "What was the crime of Expressionism? To promote the self-aggrandizement of empty words, of dead word and sound husks, which it called sensual, it turned words into mere sounds and noises, it steered the art of writing close to the cliffs of music." Cited in Roland Links, *Alfred Döblin: Leben und Werk* (Berlin: Volk und Wissen, 1976), 30.

4 "The book spells the death of real languages. The most important, creative energies of language elude the epic author who only writes." Döblin, "Der Bau des epischen Werks," 245.

5 Fassbinder shared this view: "To start with, I wanted to get a clear idea of my own obsessions while I was making films, and then I added a certain critical element to this

In the 1920s, iron curtains were raised with great frequency. The concept referred to by Döblin as epic must therefore be seen in the context of a period not lacking in appetite for reform, apodictic programs, or antagonistic emotions. Bertolt Brecht, too, labeled his theater "epic," placing this concept at the center of his program from 1930 onward. For Brecht, the epic involved a dismantling and de-hierarchization of the theater apparatus and its elements: texts, actions, gestures, speeches, stage instructions, commentary, sets, props, and lighting were treated as enunciations with equal status. The staged past was to articulate itself as an event in the present; the actor was to adopt the position of a third person or commentator with regard to his role. While the old theater had used affect in an attempt to homogenize the audience, in the new theater the audience was obliged to think, realizing its own interests, becoming polarized and partisan. So although the aesthetic impact of Brecht's method has been considerable, politicizing the audience was his overarching concern.[6]

processing of passions, and eventually I arrived at pure storytelling. A form of storytelling that contains everything, everything I think, the moral foundations, all that needs to be in there, but I don't believe the films one makes need conscious moral validation. [...] Myself, I am absolutely incapable of telling entirely flat stories. If at all, I'd only like to tell stories that I think are important to tell." Interview by Florian Hopf (1977), in Fischer, *Fassbinder über Fassbinder*, 371. And elsewhere, this time about *Berlin Alexanderplatz*: "Without this narrative compulsion the film wouldn't exist." Interview by Christian Braad Thomsen (1980), in ibid., 490. By contrast, in his assessment of *Berlin Alexanderplatz*, Thomas Elsaesser stuck more to cinematic conventions, identifying "crisis points punctuating the flow" of the narrative, which he claims "mark moments of dispersal, of energy dissipating itself in all directions, a kind of bleeding away of narrative drive, so that one only becomes aware of such critical moments in retrospect." Thomas Elsaesser, *Fassbinder's Germany: History, Identity, Subject* (Amsterdam: Amsterdam University Press, 1996), 220.

6 Firstly, by means of "literarization": "Literarizing entails punctuating 'representation' with 'formulation'; gives the theatre the possibility of making contact with other

In film, comparable approaches were developed above all in one area of Soviet cinema. Vsevolod Pudovkin and Sergei Eisenstein wanted to subvert film's illusionism by reorganizing all of the visual elements as variable signs in a new sequence. Here, too, the aesthetic program was geared toward politicization, an aim that was to be achieved primarily by a single method: montage. But such far-reaching claims were the exception in film. In its most popular forms, cinema was considered modern by default. In and of themselves, the glassy shine of its pictures, the spectacle of faces in close-up or of everyday phenomena, and the dynamism of the medium itself seemed perfect for giving expression to the modern world.

After World War II, one current within European cinema entered a phase of open modernization, with aesthetic standards that could also be derived from modernist literature. Neorealism brought new forms of generativity, friction, and tension. Unimportant instants could be drawn out, links between story units weakened in favor of cellular arrangements. It became possible to make films in which very little happened, as storylines became arbitrary, episodic, or mere pretexts. Chronologies were stretched or folded and narrative became fragmented, creating parallels to stream of consciousness.

In the 1960s, European films reached a degree of complexity hitherto seemingly reserved for other arts. People who a generation

institutions for intellectual activities; but is bound to remain one-sided so long as the audience is taking no part in it and using it as a means of obtaining access to 'higher things.'" Bertolt Brecht, "The Literarization of Theatre" (1931) in *Brecht on Theatre: The Development of an Aesthetic*, ed. John Willett (New York: Hill and Wang, 1964), 43. And secondly, via "impact": in his "Criticism of the New York Production of *The Mother*" (1935) he wrote, "Its direction requires special kinds of political knowledge and artistic capacity such as are unnecessary for the production of plays of a familiar type. [...] Drama of the *Mother* type both demands and permits a far higher degree of freedom for the sister arts, namely music and stage design, than any other type of play" (ibid., 81–82).

earlier would have been drawn to writing were now making films, and there was much overlapping and collaboration between art forms. There were also authors who moved straight into directing (Beckett, Pasolini, Robbe-Grillet, Duras, Handke) motivated by the prospect of a greater social impact, something literature was gradually beginning to lose.

At the same time, it became possible for "modernity" to be a style that shaped or reflected the aesthetic and habitual preferences of a specific audience (distance, concision, sophistication, sobriety to the point of apathy); just watching artsy and difficult productions was proof of one's cultural finesse and modernity.

In spite of this, any fundamental critique of the "apparatus" remained a rarity in film, limited to decorative traces of "reflexive" elements. Only in exceptional cases did such a critique help to shape artistic principles (immediately lending the films in question a high-cultural aura). Brecht's method was often the model here. Its influence is detectable in the films of Robert Bresson, in Alexander Kluge's ballad-like narration, in Jean-Marie Straub and Danièle Huillet's statuesque speakers and their appropriation of extraneous text material. But it was Jean-Luc Godard who took scrutiny of cinema's properties to particularly great lengths. He built cinematographic storytelling out of its core semiotic units: text, color, motion of various types, sound, words, music, and objects become autonomous enunciations. Books held in front of faces or laid over naked buttocks are also indications of an undiminished relevance of the word in print. Partaking of a more general mood of change, auteur theory with its retroactive remapping of film history made it seem realistic to put even big-budget artistic productions like feature films to more complex and demanding uses.

7 Although Godard continued to speak as a cineast, in the early 1970s he completely withdrew from productions for the cinema to work with video (during this time, he

In spite of the many shifts triggered by the French New Wave after 1960, as a by-product film also got blown up into a distinct artistic domain, in turn creating an obligation to always pay heed to the cinematic or filmic as a specific quality. For generations of filmmakers it thus became possible to refer directly and exclusively to cinematic traditions and intertexts, with a "love of cinema" as a minimal criterion for claims to artistic status. This allowed movies to become a subject of gourmet-like erudition, or to stray down the path of a dogmatism that confidently devotes itself to triviality (the repercussions of this are now being played out rather tiresomely in the films of directors like François Ozon or Quentin Tarantino).

There have of course always been exceptions to this narrow-focus cinephilia. Examples include Pasolini and Godard,[7] but also West German directors such as Herbert Achternbusch, Rosa von Praunheim, and Werner Schroeter. Hans-Jürgen Syberberg was an exception to the exception: with explicit reference to Brecht, he pushed a revisionist agenda by declaring Richard Wagner a forerunner of the film avant-garde and himself the creator of the avant-garde-film Gesamtkunstwerk.[8]

By the late 1970s, however, such positions were in decline. Not only had conditions consolidated toward a greater conformity with the market, but "modernity" had lost its positive

collaborated with Jean Rouch as a consultant on an ultimately unsuccessful project to establish a television infrastructure in Mozambique).

8 In the more advanced cinema of West Germany, the following currents can be distinguished: beginning in the 1960s, there were many attempts to reproduce the freshness of the French New Wave (*Red Sun* by Rudolf Thome, 1970, and *48 Hours to Acapulco* by Klaus Lemke, 1967). There were the abovementioned Brechtians (Kluge, Syberberg, and, to an extent, Fassbinder). While the films of Schroeter and Praunheim borrowed from the US avant-garde (Andy Warhol, the Kuchars, Jack Smith), Achternbusch worked on a regionalization of the Surrealist tradition. Important, too, was "alternative" cinema with an emancipatory agenda (Helke Sander, Praunheim).

appeal as the emphasis shifted to "retro." History films became fashionable, with the focus of interest on the 1920s and '30s and the period of Europe's various fascist regimes.[9]

Filming a Novel

This brief historical detour would have been pointless had it not been designed to establish the position of Fassbinder's *BA* and to underline two things with regard to the world of film. Firstly, this TV series would have been unthinkable without the developments in postwar European cinema discussed above. And secondly, the resulting films did not serve as models for Fassbinder, neither stylistically nor conceptually.[10]

That is not to claim that Fassbinder was the sole creator of the laws governing his work or that he determined all of the conditions under which it was made. The question of independence and authorship is not the issue here; it's just that the dependencies cannot be described in filmic terms. How far removed *BA* was from common notions of filmmaking at the time is tellingly reflected in the fact that it was produced for television. Today,

9 *The Damned* (Luchino Visconti, 1969), *The Garden of the Finzi-Continis* (Vittorio De Sica, 1970), *Cabaret* (Bob Fosse, 1972), *Lacombe, Lucien* (Louis Malle, 1974), *The Night Porter* (Liliana Cavani, 1974), *Salò, or the 120 Days of Sodom* (Pier Paolo Pasolini, 1975), *Hitler: A Film from Germany* (Hans-Jürgen Syberberg, 1977), *Mr. Klein* (Joseph Losey, 1978), etc., or the garish, pornographic films by Sergio Garrone that swam on the same tide (*SS Camp 5: Women's Hell*, 1976). A belated and intriguingly clumsy offshoot of *Cabaret* is *Just a Gigolo* by David Hemmings (1978), interesting because it features David Bowie, Kim Novak, and Marlene Dietrich in her last screen appearance.

10 With the possible exception of the aforementioned books held into the frame or of the use of title cards by Godard, although this was more in the tradition of Proletkult and Brecht. Another point is film length, which increased considerably in the 1970s: *Scenes from a Marriage* by Ingmar Bergman (1973), *1900* by Bernardo Bertolucci (1976), and *The Deer Hunter* by Michael Cimino (1978) are all around three hundred minutes; Syberberg's *Hitler* (1977) runs for 442 minutes; *Out 1* by Jacques Rivette (1971) is over twelve hours long. Fassbinder's *Berlin Alexanderplatz* outdoes them all, clocking in at over ten times the length of an average feature film.

it is hard to believe that degree to which, around 1980, discourse on film was restricted to the cinema, its history, the big screen, etc. Outside this sphere, filmmaking as an art form seemed a practical impossibility. Not only were television productions essentially ignored, they were just not taken seriously.[11]

This also makes it easier to distance *BA* from the vague category of the "filmic" and place it in the more suitable one of the "novelistic," close to the concepts of the epic developed by Brecht and Döblin. Fassbinder's film version was not only modeled on Döblin's novel in conceptual terms, the book also supplied all of its intertextual links and literary traditions: Romanticism (discontinuity of narrative elements, blending of forms, genre beyond genres, novel as theory of the novel), Naturalism (drastic portrayals of social reality, contemporary conflicts, specific milieu and modes of speech, free indirect speech), Symbolism (becoming exemplary, archaisms, "truth"), Expressionism (the new and its archaicization, the body in its organic structure and in all of its states of decay), Surrealism (abjection, paranoid perception), Nietzscheanism (repetition and eternal recurrence, concern with affects and bodily responses), as well as traces and motifs from other "avant-gardisms" that were doing the rounds at the time (anti-literature, technification of art production and factography, rejection of psychology and representation, destruction of diegetic connections by means of "montage").

A West German Critique

None of these are compatible with conventional notions of literary adaptation, which in the 1970s was also considered the least

11 This thinking persisted for a very long time in debates on the difference between film and video as material and image substrate, a difference that was accorded a positively ontological significance.

modern and least film-compatible solution. Literary adaptations were seen as a parasitic transfer of prestige into an unsuited medium, corrupting the quality of the original and the specific capacity of the film medium in equal measure.[12] And the fact that Döblin's book was to be held up as *the* German novel of the city and a literary icon of modernism made it easy to misconstrue, almost maliciously, the very elements and cultural links I have highlighted in favor of Fassbinder's approach.

This widespread hostility is summed up by the literary critic Heinz Brüggemann, whose text was one of the few non-journalistic pieces on Fassbinder's *BA* to appear at the time in West Germany. In spite of its academic character, it shares certain biases expressed in the journalistic reviews, and it has the advantage of both thoroughness and a knowledge of the text.[13]

Brüggemann diligently compared passages from Döblin's novel with Fassbinder's script. Although this is a logical-enough approach, it was done with the unmistakable aim of presenting the film version in an unfavorable light. Once again, melodrama was cited as the epitome of dreadful and vulgar pop culture. Fassbinder was charged with having normalized and re-psychologized Döblin's "modernity," "ruthlessly reducing it to human relations," thus "opposing the modernity, aesthetic

12 This concern with faithfulness to the original work is rarely encountered today, even where it might actually be appropriate, as in the current wave of stage adaptations of novels and even movies at German theaters.

13 Heinz Brüggemann, "*Berlin Alexanderplatz* oder 'Franz, Mieze, Reinhold, Tod & Teufel'? R. W. Fassbinders filmische Lektüre des Romans von Döblin" [*Berlin Alexanderplatz* or 'Franz, Mieze, Reinhold, death & devil'? R. W. Fassbinder's filmic reading of the novel by Döblin], *text + kritik*, no. 103 (July 1989): 51–65. Fassbinder's reception in Germany is a many-sided and somewhat sad topic, but there is not space enough to deal with it here. Nothing could be easier, however, than to provide evidence of the crudeness of well-meaning contemporary film critics who never went beyond received ideas, imprecise use of categories, and anodyne attributions. In addition, due to Fassbinder's diverse fields of activity, discussion of his work was spread across the journalistically separate territories

radicalism, and cold-bloodedness of the original by all available means." The human individual was returned here to the very representational space and subject constructs that Döblin had set out to destroy. And, in the film, the actors were made to say what the novel had conveyed via montage. Brüggemann clearly compared the two works from the position of someone much enamored with a bold, domineering, and militant modernism. In 1989—several years after the director's death—this prompted the critic to offer the following schoolmasterly verdict: "A film adaptation of the novel should first have familiarized itself with its cinematic style and then attempted to engage productively with this formal idiom."

Of course it is possible to track down omissions, shifts, and additions in Fassbinder's film, and the call for an appropriate rendering is anything but mistaken. But it is easy enough to imagine the film that would have better satisfied such requirements—somewhere between Eisenstein, Hans Richter, Dziga Vertov, and Godard, with a jittering touch of Walter Ruttmann and some tumbling perspective lines à la Rodchenko.

All in all, Brüggemann presupposed the value of Döblin's novel as a firm given, playing it off as such against Fassbinder's film.[14] But however this assessment of the novel may have come

of television, theater, and cinema. One of the few pieces that also dealt with methods was Peter Iden's "Der Eindruck-Macher: Rainer Werner Fassbinder und das Theater" [The impression-maker: Rainer Werner Fassbinder and the theater, 1975]—tellingly, this was a text by a theater critic about Fassbinder's work for the stage; in *Rainer Werner Fassbinder*, ed. Peter W. Jansen and Wolfram Schütte, 5th rev. ed. (Munich: Hanser, 1985), 17–28. Most tellingly, the most accurate remarks on Fassbinder's films are from the margins: some of the best and most clear-sighted came from Werner Schroeter, included in the bonus materials on the DVD of *In a Year of 13 Moons*.

14 As far as I am concerned, it was Fassbinder's film that paved the way into Döblin's *BA*. Without the film, I would have seen Döblin's often witty gruffness, his deliberate bluntness, and his pithy irony as merely the crude bluster of a special German expressivity. Without Fassbinder, the novel's finer points would have all but escaped me.

about, its standing has never been entirely unchallenged. On its original publication in 1929, the response was divided along clear lines: while it received generally favorable reviews in the bourgeois press, the organs of German communism gave it a rougher ride. The reviewers in *Rote Fahne* and *Die Linkskurve* were especially unanimous in their rejection, crying out: The working class betrayed! This is not how proletarians speak! This is not our Alexanderplatz! Reality is not how this left-wing bourgeois author imagines it! What a deliberate distortion in terms of class! And far too abstract!

Some of the reviews of Döblin in 1930 uncannily resembled those later received by Fassbinder: "In his book, Döblin has dressed the battered ego of a complicated petit-bourgeois in proletarian garb."[15] Johannes R. Becher, who went on to occupy high official positions in East Germany after the war, delivered an early and especially creepy example of a condescending and aggressive officiousness that left no doubt about who was master over the meaning and aims of art: "We affirm the possibility of a proletarian-revolutionary literature even before the proletariat takes power. [...] Over the last two years, our proletarian-revolutionary writing has progressed strongly. Our books have proved that they, too, are weapons in the class struggle," etc.[16] From this wave of progress he explicitly excepted Döblin's *BA*, crowing: "Literary high treason!"[17] (This was

15 Otto Biha, "Herr D verunglückt in einer Linkskurve" [Herr D crashes in a left turn], *Die Linkskurve* 2, no. 6 (1930), quoted in *Materialien zu Alfred Döblin "Berlin Alexanderplatz"*, ed. Matthias Prangel (Frankfurt am Main: Suhrkamp, 1975), 98.

16 Johannes R. Becher, "Einen Schritt weiter!" [One step further!], *Die Linkskurve* 2, no. 1 (1930), quoted in ibid., 88.

17 Ibid., 89. Elsewhere, too, "proletarian art" was ruthlessly defended, the accusations forming part of a campaign to prevent the translation of *BA* into Russian. The report began as follows: "Notice from the editorial staff of *Die Linkskurve*: Herr Döblin is to be struck off." *Die Linkskurve* 2, no. 10 (1930), in ibid., 100.

hardly surprising considering Biberkopf's subproletarian status, the antidogmatic stance of *BA*, and the way that, on a metaphorical level, Döblin slyly refutes claims made for the proletarian as a historical subject: Biberkopf is run over by the wheels that would stand still if his strong arm wanted them to—if he had work, that is—and if his arm had not been crushed by these wheels.)[18]

While the historical materialist of 1930 positioned his notions based on the realist novel of the nineteenth century against Döblin's montage technique, the materialist of 1989 defended this same technique, accused of formalism in 1930, against Fassbinder's film version. Something originally at odds with this politicized art doctrine was later heartily embraced by it. Although on closer inspection such discussions of incompatible concepts of realism appear justified, they also bear vivid witness to a dogmatism that, in the name of higher or established values, always validates precisely that which is not the case. But a knowing smirk would be misplaced here were it based on the assumption that the present is spared such vicious circles or that one is not caught up in them oneself.

After World War II, Döblin himself did not fare much better. The sad facts of emigration and the attendant disruption of his writing were followed by the experience of a failed return to Germany.[19] [TALES OF A LONG NIGHT] A turning point in the

18 Part of the metaphorical resonance is parodic, referring to a traditional slogan of the German labor movement: "All wheels stand still / If it is your will."

19 Döblin returned to Germany with the French occupying forces. He was a co-founding member of the German Academy of Language and Literature in Darmstadt, and continued to publish. From the outset, however, his political ambitions in the field of art could hardly be put into practice, and after the currency union of 1949 they were further obstructed, in some cases by old Nazis. He wrote about this situation in a letter to Ludwig Marcuse in August 1951: "You haven't missed anything by staying in America. How things are going here, in terms of domestic politics, you can see for yourself, dear Marcuse.

assessment of his work did not come until 1967, with an essay by Günter Grass.[20]

Montage

The mixture of views concerning Döblin was matched by the range of opinion concerning the value and function of "montage." For Brüggemann, it was the hypertrophic signifier of a modernity awash with violent metaphors (blast, confrontation, radicality, shock). In his review of *BA*, Walter Benjamin wrote: "The stylistic principle governing this book is that of montage. Petit-bourgeois printed matter, scandal-mongering, stories of accidents, the sensational incidents of 1928, folk songs, and advertisements rain down in this text. The montage explodes the framework of the novel, bursts its limits both stylistically and structurally, and clears the way for new, epic possibilities. Formally, above all. The material of the montage is by no means arbitrary. Authentic montage is based on the document."[21]

Never in Germany have we had such a political situation, purely nationalistic and unfree, reactionary, as we have now. The Socialists are certainly no left-wing party. The old middle class is done for, the writers are opportunists, intellectually of no importance and impregnated more or less deeply with Nazi ideas. If you spend any length of time here, you will feel the alien and hostile air. I am no longer young enough, otherwise I would have departed on my second, definitive emigration as much as two years ago." In *Doppelleben: Literarische Szenen aus Nachkriegsdeutschland*, ed. Helmut Böttiger, Thomas Combrink, and Bernd Busch (Göttingen: Wallstein, 2009), 262.

20 Günter Grass, "Döblin, My Teacher" (1967), in *On Writing and Politics: 1967–1983* (San Diego: Harcourt Brace Jovanovich, 1985), 3–24.

21 Benjamin, "Crisis of the Novel," 301. He then wished to make this the founding principle of his own work, too. Of *The Arcades Project*, he wrote: "Method of this work: literary montage. I needn't *say* anything. Merely show. I shall purloin no valuables, appropriate no ingenious formulations. But the rags, the refuse—these I will not inventory but allow, in the only way possible, to come into their own: by making use of them." Walter Benjamin, "Convolute N: On the Theory of Knowledge, Theory of Progress," in *The Arcades Project* (Cambridge, MA: Harvard University Press, 1999), N1a8, p. 460.

Adorno refuted this view, considering the principle of montage as a source of acute danger. The threat, as he saw it, was to the status of the artwork itself. For Adorno, art formulates its own laws within the means of its appearance, defining both the limits of these means and the repertoire of "formal problems" to be solved. In his view, the most progressive art corresponds to society as a whole, brought forth *as* art, in that art's distinct form, and under its own unique conditions.

Montage attacks this logic on two fronts. Firstly, its inclusion of extraneous material imposes on art the wrong themes and problems. Secondly, it speeds up the descent into lawlessness and formlessness: "Montage amounts to the disruption, and hence the denial, of meaning in works of art through the invasion of fragments of empirical reality that do not abide by the laws of art. The erosion of the arts is almost always accompanied by the attempt by works of art to reach out toward an extra-aesthetic reality."[22]

Since the principle of montage was the seminal example of this "fraying" of art,[23] leading to "invasions" (of unprocessed material drawn from "reality"), the autonomy of art is hollowed out, causing the "particular, socially reserved sphere of art" to be subjugated, alienating art production from its true tasks and

22 Theodor W. Adorno, "Art and the Arts" (1967), in Theodor W. Adorno, *Can One Live after Auschwitz? A Philosophical Reader*, ed. Rolf Tiedemann, trans. Rodney Livingstone et al. (Stanford, CA: Stanford University Press, 2003), 385. André Bazin, too, saw montage as an act of violence that destroyed the potential ambiguity of the film image. He contrasted this with *durée* and the long shot: these allow the gaze to wander, leave sense and meaning open, and install the "montage" within the shot itself. Bazin saw this as a profoundly "liberal" and "democratic" approach. Moreover, when a long shot is paired with depth of focus, "concrete reality" is left to its own devices, preserving its genuine dignity. The "filmic" of the 1920s had become the "un-filmic" of the 1950s.

23 Here we deliberately used a more literal translation of the German *Verfransung*, not the published rendering as "erosion" in the preceding quote. (*Trans.*)

problems.[24] By forfeiting its autonomy, art also loses the ability to address societal contradictions in model form, in a different material, and using a different mode of production. (One should not attempt to portray something using that thing itself as one's material.) If one abandons this special zone's freedom from purpose and interests, one has nothing left to set against an immediacy that, presumptuous and terroristic as it is, ultimately does nothing but smooth out contradictions and discontinuities. In the end, this hands a victory to all that is illusionary, conformist, and industrially preformatted (ninety minutes for a feature film, four minutes for a song). Again and again, Adorno uses the word "kitsch."

At the end of the 1960s, precisely such claims regarding the function of art were massively criticized in the United States, where Clement Greenberg's positions epitomized a newly reactionary modernism before coming in for widespread condemnation. Although based on painting, Greenberg's "standards of excellence" overlap with Adorno's views on art (immanence, specificity, autonomy, high-art appeal), and the central charge of a one-sided view of modern art, blocking out its "productionist" elements, can also be leveled against them both.

For Adorno, the mass-oriented feature film was an example of "fraying" in its most despicable, idiotic, and brutal form. Had he had his way, it would not have been necessary (or even possible) to take films into account in a scenario of progress that was in any way relevant. Although he did occasionally admit the possibility of "emancipatory," enlightening cinema, he also failed to see it even where it had already emerged before his very eyes. In this light, it is almost paradoxical that the Frankfurt

24 Theodor W. Adorno, *Philosophy of New Music*, ed. and trans. Robert Hullot-Kentor (Minneapolis: University of Minnesota Press, 2006), 13.

School had such a decisive influence on West German film criticism, supplying its more rigorous factions with concepts, political demands, and figures of thought (context of delusion, reification, purposive rationality, dictate of profit, false consciousness, alienation).[25]

Under such conditions, it is not surprising that in 1980, it was practically and theoretically difficult to see in Fassbinder's *BA* a distinct artistic movement, not to mention identifying in its baroque appeal anything "advanced," a coherent concept of realism, or something akin to a method. Even today, it is not easy to reconcile the production's secondhand prewar Berlin (the street scenes were filmed on sets from Ingmar Bergman's *The Serpent's Egg* that had recently been shot at Munich's Bavaria Studios), mouth-organ soundtrack, worn-out wardrobe, and barricaded, grotto-like interiors with a "crystalline," progressive modernism that spiritedly hacked its material to pieces. But all of this also made it more difficult still to see the film's productive and "modern" dimension precisely in this backward-looking, old-style approach and its strong sense of theatricality.

Or, to put it differently (and to jump ahead a little): with critical tools of this kind, it was never going to be possible to properly grasp or to embrace a constellation where "alienation" is affirmed, where truth is sought in "false consciousness," and whose concept of the subject positively relies on the "context of delusion."

25 This influence can be felt, for example, through to the small mannerism of placing the reflexive pronoun directly in front of the corresponding verb, as often found in the writing of Frieda Grafe—who, incidentally, also had little to say about Fassbinder's films. The same applies to the film magazine *Filmkritik*, an authoritative German voice on cinema since the 1960s, which, even in its late period at the end of the 1970s (and regardless of the battles between the camps of an "aesthetic Left" and a "political Left") reacted to Fassbinder's films, if at all, with open hostility, offering anonymous but high-handed pieces of advice like the following: "You better start learning how to make movies first."

The thinking at work here had no place for the diligent reproduction of notions of transparency, immanence, and discontinuity. Instead, its focus lay elsewhere, and its range was far greater. Fassbinder left the original largely intact, retelling a story already told by Döblin, taking on all of its elements and themes, as well as their connections and connotations, in an act of appropriation.

Filming the Appropriation of a Novel

It would not be misleading to make the link to appropriation art and its Duchampian vector here. In fine art, similar debates on authorship, artistic autonomy, and the dialectic of original and copy were conducted at more or less the same time.[26] But unlike Fassbinder, this generation of American artists was not only explicitly influenced by French post-structuralist theory, their works were also received against this same background. Every artistic utterance was now a "social text" (in Kristeva's words), "allegorical" (in Benjamin's), or (in Barthes's) the effect of an endless chain of readings. (This climate of openness to post-structuralist notions was also the reason why Fassbinder's films were more adequately received in the United States than they were in the director's own country.)

But although Fassbinder had worked in the same mode of intertwined readings, his historicization of modernism aimed in a different direction. He, too, drew his material of choice into a dialectical movement of repetition, displacement, and sublation, but in *BA* he did not share the taste for inauthentic ways of enunciation that was widespread in the 1980s.[27] Irony and parody play no part here, nor does usurpation or fixation on

26 Fassbinder had already raised these questions in *Satan's Brew* (1976)—a poet overcomes a bout of writer's block by accidentally writing a poem by Stefan George, itself "inspired" by Baudelaire.

intrinsic art discourses. For Fassbinder, there was no reason to grate against possible deficits and presumptions of modernism. He wanted neither to reassess nor devalue Döblin's novel. Instead, he took it fully on board as a resource, with all of its parts and because of them—as the point of departure for a way of thinking that repeats someone else's way of thinking. In this way, it was possible for Döblin's "modernity" to become Fassbinder's archaism. Conversely, this allowed him to see the old even in the new, to "allegorize" the present day of 1980, and to historicize literary modernism. Fassbinder was connected to a post-structuralist, "French" vector of thinking because in the 1920s, one might say, this "French" vector had a precocious "German" equivalent.[28]

27 German film critics were all but blind to Fassbinder's artistic procedures. It took a theater critic to get their relevance somewhat right. Of his production of Goldoni's *The Coffee Shop* (Bremen, 1969), Peter Iden wrote, "Everything about this adaptation and its staging is play on other plays, performance of other performances." This was not meant as a compliment. Iden found the production contrived, incoherent, and overly "disparate" in its distribution of voices. In spite of this, he did identify a method. In addition, he was able to decipher references down to the details of gestures and elements of the stage set: many were taken from a production of *Torquato Tasso* by Peter Stein that had recently taken place at the same theater. See Jansen and Schütte, *Rainer Werner Fassbinder*, 22.

28 Which would even confirm what Douglas Crimp wrote in 1993, looking back on the debate surrounding modernism and postmodernism in America: "The practices I claimed as postmodernist seemed to me to continue the unfinished avant-garde project. Indeed, the prewar avant-garde appeared, through the lens of a postmodernism critical of modernism, virtually as postmodernism *avant la lettre*." Douglas Crimp, *On the Museum's Ruins* (Cambridge, MA: MIT Press, 1993), 19.

Using Machines to Make This Peculiar Thing We Call an Image

> Sirk has said you can't make films about something, you can only make films with something.
>
> This work of art, *Berlin Alexanderplatz*, also helps you get a theoretical handle on things without itself being theoretical.
>
> —Rainer W. Fassbinder

What *is* film? And what is *a* film? Film studies and film criticism usually privilege the visual level of movies and refer to their visual side as the image. Within the overall arrangement of audiovisual acts, this level is the main focus, occasionally also referred to as the "thinking" image, while focusing on merely pictorial qualities. If one assumes that the key to *BA* as a film lies in its novel-like quality and the abovementioned mimetic strategy, then this also implies that it cannot be fully explained in terms of cinematographic evidence, laws, or syntax alone.

This being the case, a film, too, could be subject to the logic that prompted Döblin to break the "literary" mold by means of the epic. In turn, this would mean that modernist notions like media propriety or the dependence of an utterance on its linguistic structure would not apply.

This does not, of course, render it unnecessary to discuss *BA* as a film. There is no denying that Fassbinder's work presents itself to us as a film (even as a 16 mm film made for television), and it certainly offers material that never was and never could have been written in the book. Nonetheless, it would be pointless or restrictive to cling to the visual properties of the work, granting them primary status in order to establish so-called visual strategies or a politics of the image on the basis of which everything else might then be unlocked.

The Ultraphotographic

Although film has outstandingly direct access to the plenitude of the world, it was noted early on that the film image creates not only likenesses, but also mixed and ambiguous conglomerates. The impact of combining two visual elements to achieve an accumulation of associations is always both physiological and intellectual (Sergei Eisenstein). The image stands between the written or spoken word (Raymond Bellour). Film is based on "ultraphotographic interventions"; joining two images does not result in an image; the visual chain of the film resembles the chain of writing (Albert Laffay). A similar view was taken by German narratologists of the 1950s: "The animated picture, which exercises a narrative function, brings the film closer to epic than to dramatic fiction. When we see a film we are viewing narrated material, a novel" (Käte Hamburger).[1]

In his film theory, Gilles Deleuze, too, discussed ambiguous articulations, particularly in connection with what he calls the perception-image: "There is no mixture or average of two subjects, each belonging to a system, but a differentiation of two correlative subjects in a system which is itself heterogeneous."[2]

What does this mean? Deleuze amalgamates two narrative techniques that have little in common but that nonetheless amount to something similar: "free indirect speech" and "mise en abyme." In both cases, two elements are combined into a third.

1 Käte Hamburger, *The Logic of Literature* (1957), trans. Marilynn J. Rose (Bloomington: Indiana University Press, 1973), 222.

Free indirect speech is a mode of portraying speech in narrative texts that Deleuze became aware of through Pasolini's writings on film theory (I will come back to this). The concept of the mise en abyme was devised by André Gide through an analogy with a feature in heraldry in order to describe a specific narrative construction based on nesting. Just as a coat of arms may include figures or symbols that are repeated in miniature form, one level of the narrative is reflected in another. In Gide's *Paludes* (1895), a writer writes a novel entitled *Paludes* and discusses the poetological assumptions on which it is based. Thirty years later, Gide repeated this exercise: *The Counterfeiters* is a novel that includes details of the failed project of writing a "pure novel."[3]

The crystalline form of Gide's mises en abyme is achieved by nesting circles of consciousness and levels of knowledge, a structure that refracts the light cast on individual characters. With regard to film, Deleuze inferred the following from mise en abyme and free indirect speech: "It is a case of going beyond the subjective and the objective towards a pure form which sets itself up as an autonomous vision of the content. We are no longer faced with subjective *or* objective images; we are caught in the correlation between a perception-image and a camera-consciousness which transforms it (the question of whether the image was objective or subjective is no longer raised). It is a

2 Gilles Deleuze, *Cinema 1: The Movement-Image*, trans. Hugh Tomlinson and Barbara Habberjam (Minneapolis: University of Minnesota Press, 1986), 73.

3 Edouard, the main character: "To tell the truth, of the actual book not a line has been written. [...] Day by day in a note-book, I note the state of the novel in my mind. [...] Instead of contenting myself with resolving each difficulty as it presents itself (and every work of art is only the sum or the product of the solutions of a quantity of small difficulties), I set forth each of these difficulties and study it." Then, more defiantly: "The history of the book [...] interested me more than the book itself." André Gide, *The Counterfeiters* (1927), trans. Dorothy Bussy (New York: Vintage, 1973), 189. This can also be seen as an early form of Conceptualism.

very special kind of cinema which has acquired a taste for 'making the camera felt.'"[4] The last turn of phrase is taken from Pasolini, as is the example of this "feelability" Deleuze gives: a person walks out of the frame, but the camera lingers.

Where Gide intended to illustrate a particular storytelling device, Deleuze took these narrative elements as a basis for conclusions about visual elements, and more specifically about certain image compositions. In Deleuze's mise en abyme, then, the camera is elevated to the status of a "higher" authority that regulates access to a film's narrative text and the way this text refers to itself—not only in individual works, but also within a group of films on the same level of ambitiousness. With this transposition from a literary to a visual faculty, the focus shifted onto "perception." The perception-image "doubles the perception of an independent aesthetic consciousness. [...] The perception-image finds its status, as free indirect subjective, from the moment that it reflects its content in a camera consciousness which has become autonomous."[5]

This last point is also an example of certain dead ends in film theory resulting from a fixation on visual or media categories. Although Deleuze's books on cinema sought primarily to ground a film-theoretical approach in philosophical thinking, they were also heir to the blossoming of attempts in the 1960s to establish sets of rules and "syntagmas" that could be applied to each and every film.

Feature films are supremely elastic and derivative, however, making it hard to define where rules end and exceptions begin. Generalizations also fail to distinguish between films one finds interesting, uninteresting, interesting only in details, or not *as* films. On the other hand, not everyone can afford such a magni-

4 Deleuze, *Cinema 1*, 74.

5 Ibid.

ficent anti-academicism as Félix Guattari, or express views on cinema as succinctly and vehemently as he does. For him, a motion picture is a "complex semiotic orchestration," its "heterogeneous traits of the matter of expression," in which not everything is "simply a discourse," but shows fascinating "intensities of all kinds, constellations of features of faciality, crystallizations of affects" that, as a kind of cinematic unconscious, induce a "vertigo of abolition." A movie is a carnival for which one pays so as "to be invaded by subjective arrangements with blurry contours, in order to give in to adventures that, in principle, have no lasting effects."[6]

In the Image of BA

As far as the film *BA* is concerned, I must underline again that it cannot be understood purely in terms of its visual properties or some "filmic" self-evidence. And, for that matter, Fassbinder's refusal to grant ultimate priority to the visual is clearly marked in *BA*: by acoustic overloading of perception, but mainly by the darkening of the scenes (which was completely unacceptable to audiences at the time). By denying material to the sense of sight and often delegating it to the ear, he raised a strong objection to demands for a clear view into the image itself. Another noteworthy feature is *BA*'s lack of the gestures of media self-referentiality that were widely used by other auteur directors at the time (film projections within films, optical instruments). Or rather, he established a different and very telling kind of referent: a large printing machine in Biberkopf's sublet room that would be an obtuse prop with no diegetic force if it didn't point to "the book" as the film's formative sphere.

6 Félix Guattari, "The Poor Man's Couch" (1975), in *Chaosophy: Texts and Interviews, 1972–1977,* ed. Sylvère Lotringer, trans. David L. Sweet, Jarred Becker, and Taylor Adkins (Los Angeles: Semiotext(e), 2009), 263–65.

It would be going too far, however, to see Fassbinder as an iconoclast and enemy of the optical in general. After all, touches of extravagance, sleekness, and high-handedness in the field of photographic rendering and cinematic design are the trademarks of his work. Following a brief phase of deliberately sparse, frontal long takes, he soon switched to convoluted camera choreographies, mirrors, and the use of spaces and images barricaded by pillars, door jambs, and window frames. These multiple framings were matched by the splitting up of audiovisual levels, most extremely in *The Third Generation*, *In a Year of 13 Moons*, and *Querelle*, but also in *BA*.

As Fassbinder was neither fussy nor fundamentalist, his technical solutions are always tied to specific situations, the exploration of feasibilities, the impact of haste, or the economics of filmmaking in budgetary terms. This is also why many of his films feel patchy, even by the standards of their time. Film-theoretical generalizations are also made more difficult by the fact that he worked in different genres, modes, and media.

What, for example, would a systematizing or even semiotic approach make of this scene in *BA*/2: Biberkopf is working as a street vendor, selling tie clips from a table in front of a window display of wedding dresses. During the shot, the camera position switches twice, plainly enough, to the interiors of nearby stores, where the same scene is now filmed through shop windows and their displays. As a result, various objects appear in the foreground: a pair of silk shoes, then a plucked chicken strung up by its feet. If shots always had to be attributable to a clear point of view, then this one would appear arbitrary or inconsistent.[7]

However, something that goes against the rules may, firstly, be of no importance or, secondly, prove revelatory nonetheless. As well as erratic points of view, the sequence also features an abrupt and brief layering of unrelated elements. The resulting "montages" might be the beginnings of chains of metaphor deserving further exploration (chicken, shoe, wedding dress—slaughter, physical movement, ostentatious display of social or gender norms), or they might mean nothing at all.

Within Fassbinder's visual idiom, a more consistent and effective role is certainly played by mirrors. Looking in the mirror, characters confirm the visible aspect of their identity, the front view of a body that appears in coherent unity. At the level of the film image, however, mirrors create dissociations and secondary frames—with visual blocks potentially adding third or fourth ones—whose implications only become clear to the viewer: the mirror paints captivity in one's own body and mind as the cage of identity.[8]

Shaping Figures

But whatever status such interventions accord to the camera, it is still only one aspect within an overall structure shaped by many other factors. Perhaps, however, if one doesn't define "concept" too narrowly, even Fassbinder's use of actors can be described as conceptual—although he didn't go as far as some modernist filmmakers. There is not the kind of programmatic framing developed by Eisenstein (figure as sign), Bresson (figure as "model"), or Straub/Huillet (figure as speaker of text).

7 This sequence is by no means an exception. For Elsaesser, who is frequently annoyed by the director's lack of cinematographic propriety, such inconsistencies are in fact a trademark of Fassbinder's filmmaking. His evaluation of *BA*: "A complex and cluttered visual space even by Fassbinder's standards allows the camera to inscribe a peculiarly unsettling look, obtrusive in that it is often attributable only to secondary figures, and sometimes to no on-screen character at all." Elsaesser, *Fassbinder's Germany*, 219.

8 This is confirmed by what Fassbinder said in interviews when asked about mirrors, calling the space they create "bourgeois" and their function in his films "to create distance," "impede identification," and "generate alienation." Interviews by John Hughes and Brooks Riley (1975), and Limmer/Rumler (1980), in *Fassbinder über Fassbinder*, 352, 535–36.

Fassbinder's method was based above all on externalizing the portrayal of emotions and reducing their intensity, sometimes to the point of apathy. Even the most agitated states are performed via mechanical gestures and facial expressions, in contrast to today's binary standard of expressiveness (introverted/extroverted). This mechanical physicality is affirmed and reinforced by its correlation with the approach to framing as elements in a choreography. The best-known example of such an arrangement is the inward-facing circular tracking shot in *Martha* (a device also used several times in *BA*). Its disorientating and dizzying impact is due to a threefold movement—along with the orbiting concentric pan of the camera, the two actors rotate around each other, and on their own axis, while maintaining eye contact.[9]

What is true of these camera/body choreographies can be applied to the gaze in general. In Fassbinder's films, eyes never imitate natural ways of looking or seeing. As in the feature films of the classic period, looks have a gestural function, being just one relational element among others.[10] Taken together, these measures reflect Fassbinder's understanding of social structures. Everything is conceived of in terms of relations, and nothing outside of this is provided for. (Which may explain be why his films contain almost no unrelated images, no "im-

9 Here, too, we are not dealing with "inventions." Although Fassbinder never referred to Max Ophüls's films, there are striking similarities, not least on the level of camera work: the barricading of spaces and a preference for curving and circling camera movements. In some scenes by Ophüls, as in *Lola Montès* (1955), the movement patterns appear just as deliberately overloaded: drifting or rotating cameras occasionally correlate with counterrotating podiums or actors.

10 Today, by contrast, actors are made to resemble actual human beings as plausibly as possible, which seems to promote mannerisms of "intensity" like exaggerated liveliness, expressions of disapproval, minute twitches of facial muscles, etc. In the course of this development the function of the gaze in films has changed completely. The gaze is no longer a hinge and object; instead, the eye becomes an entry or exit hole, circling in and around its own distinctiveness as a marker of the greatest psychological intensity. As

pressions" or still lives, no cheeky takes on urban street life, "wacky characters," or conspicuous behavior.)

A central and conceptually significant part is played here by Fassbinder's understanding of the pose. Since his early works for screen and stage, his attention to this was evident (as in his production of Goldoni's *The Coffee Shop*, which has survived as a recording for television). Gestures and poses inscribe into the body what might be called a historical dimension that takes the form of "attitude." The inside of a pose consists in an exteriority that is connected with what Thomas Mann once called "lived myth." Based on this understanding, a pose is not the arbitrary expression of some private ceremony, but an appropriating embodiment of a preordained sequence (making it the physical equivalent of Fassbinder's other forms of appropriation). One such gesture is repeated especially often by male characters in Fassbinder's films, signaling melancholy, homosexuality, "femininity": the palm of the left hand is rested on the right shoulder and the head inclined toward it.

Although films are not the only source here, they must nonetheless be taken into account as referents. If nothing else, they provided models for crass stereotypes of gender-specific behavior. In contrast to Brecht or the modernist filmmakers mentioned above, Fassbinder did not restrict his syntheses to character, role, and speech, introducing gender and sexuality as a decisive factor. An outstanding example of this is the non-essentialist, antimimetic rendering of a transgender figure in *In a Year of 13 Moons*, where the tall and bulky body of Volker

a result, offensive and super-clear looking to the point of staring becomes the dominant mode in face depictions and close-ups, ranging from "assertive aggressiveness" to "thorough thoughtfulness." This type of gaze not only reflects everyday styles of self-assertion, but also affirms them. On this level, too, a positive charge is given to self-will, cleverness, and an insistence on the ego. In American productions, this is on the wane, but not in German ones. [GERMAN CALAMITIES (1980–2010)]

Spengler is scaled back to very small, gentle gestures and a whispery voice.

The expressive tools actively used by Fassbinder, especially in *BA*, include a differentiated range of speech patterns and tones of voice, various dialects, and other kinds of strongly colored German (including Yiddish). In Fassbinder's work, even such a pragmatic move as foregoing the live sound so beloved of many modernist filmmakers reinforces the dissociative quality. In his early films a willfully paradoxical mixing of voices occurred: one actor is dubbed by another member of the cast, who in turn is dubbed by a third, and so forth. Moreover, different performance styles or schools of acting, including the use of amateurs, create collisions of their own (this is in fact true of any fictional film). Fassbinder favored an affected, breathy style of vocal delivery, as associated with German theater, cinema, and radio plays into the 1960s, contributed mainly by actresses—in *BA*, specifically Annemarie Düringer and Margit Carstensen.

And as we are talking about the "semiotic" function of Fassbinder's actors, we must of course mention his casting stunt of bringing in meaning generated elsewhere: famous actors from family series or sex films, stars of 1950s West German cinema, East Germany, and the Nazi period. As well as having important ties to Germany's provincial theaters, Fassbinder always cast friends, his mother, various lovers, and people from his immediate professional milieu. In later films, he increasingly used internationally known actors for leading roles. Often enough, however, this brought a collapse of nuance and a dulling of reference (in *Despair* and *Querelle* respectively, Dirk Bogarde and Jeanne Moreau are mere shadows of themselves).

As a final aside here, "conceptualism" or "dissociation" does not mean willfully withdrawing from reality. Fassbinder's films clearly show that a lessening of realistic impact can lead to a heightened sense of realism. One need only think, for example, of the striking spectrum of characters and social types to be found in his work.

Using Machines

Now, if we cannot define film as a whole, it might still be good, more specifically, to find a fitting term for what *BA* actually *is*, both within and beyond its particular modes of signification. The concept of the epic already implied a broader, intermedia type of configuration. But epic sounds so very ancient and heavy. Fassbinder once compared his oeuvre to a house. Benjamin called Döblin's epic "oceanic." Perhaps a term from another sphere would be better suited?

In the twentieth century, technical terms were standard metaphorical fare, especially "machine" (Freud, Vertov, Duchamp, Picabia, Warhol, Roussel, Deleuze/Guattari, etc.). Conceived of as a voracious, autonomous metabolism, however, this metaphor is less valuable when applied to film, overdetermined by the fact that films actually do have an electromechanical basis. In this light, the apparatus in Jean-Louis Baudry's "apparatus theory" is just another example of excessive analogy, in this case between the apparatus of the cinema and Freud's mental apparatus, which Freud famously compared to a camera obscura. Among others, this analogy was excessive in that the film-specific identifications, the reception of films in general, and the impact of fiction in particular were explained only in terms of their technical setup. But as we now know, the narrative potential of audiovisual sequences does not depend on the constellation of projector, row of seats, screen, and paralysis of the body in the dark, especially not in the case of a television series.[11]

11 The assumptions of this theoretical position, which were in use for some time, have long since infiltrated the way everyday life is understood. In today's praxis of

A different metaphor is needed here, then—but I can't think of one. Many of the incidental or occasional definitions given here seem to boil down to Michel Foucault's *dispositif*. It is perfectly possible to describe films in keeping with his description as "decidedly heterogeneous ensembles." But as used in the context of (German) film theory, as an update for apparatus, dispositif forfeits its aspect of multidimensional deployment: the networked organization of the dispositif centers on issues of power, authority, and government. A single film, even such an unusually long one, is too "small" and not "powerful" enough—and the same probably applies to cinema or television as a medium or institution. A film can be part of a dispositif, but it cannot be the dispositif itself. Moreover, Foucault's concept is not suited to describing artistic procedures or the specific form in which they manifest themselves. It might be possible to draw on Deleuze's take on the concept: a mixed ensemble of images and utterances that shed light on objects and contexts, and vice versa. An incidental remark by Deleuze is in fact even better suited, and although it narrows the radius of the definition, it has the advantage of a suggestive echo (Bresson). In a text on Foucault, Deleuze defined dispositifs as "machines which make one see and speak."[12] This making see / letting speak is not exactly a definition, but the minimum requirement for impact it implies is good enough for now, at least as a cursory description of function.

art education, "apparatus theory" is put into action on a day-to-day basis. The sinking cost of projection equipment has led to many and varied forms of presentation for moving images, but the reception of this ubiquitous phenomenon is now "conceptual," focusing far more strongly on contexts and identifications with the apparatus than on individual works or their specific character. [Exhibiting a Movie]

12 Gilles Deleuze, "What Is a *Dispositif*?" (1988), in *Michel Foucault, Philosopher: Essays Translated from the French and German*, ed. and trans. Timothy J. Armstrong (London: Routledge, 1992), 160. Bresson's take was conceived of more in terms of

film itself: "Problem. To make what you see be seen, through the intermediary of a machine that does not see it as you see it. And to make heard what you hear, through the intermediary of another machine that does not hear it as you do." Robert Bresson, *Notes on the Cinematographer*, trans. Jonathan Griffin (New York: Urizen Books, 1977), 37.

Which Social Perspective, and How?

> Viewed as a whole, the German novel of today doesn't go beyond the framework of petit-bourgeois and bourgeois intellectual concerns.
> —Walter Benjamin, in an interview

> The lives of others, what could that be?
> —René Pollesch

Ordinarily, film adaptations of literary works pay little heed to such definitions of impact and function, riding roughshod over even the simplest mental or theoretical activities contained in the original. And if a costume drama is called for, then a picturesque result is truly inevitable. While pretending to fill the past with life then, what we usually find marinating in the movie is whatever is most at odds with the written fiction of the source. Döblin's novel certainly offers scope for cuts and contractions, but his feverish evocations of the city, in particular, seem to cry out for minute reconstruction nonetheless. [Berlin Super-City] Fassbinder not only did not fulfill such expectations, he turned them into their opposite: glassy modernism into Rembrandt-esque golden brown, parataxis into hypotaxis, abrupt angularity into sensitive smoothness, "metropolis" into studio interiors. And finally, he increased the average age of Döblin's cast so significantly that, even on this level, exuberance was effectively ruled out.

Fassbinder, too, sometimes seemed guilty of heedlessness. In an essay on *BA*, he repeatedly emphasized a positively existential affinity with his source material ("I am Biberkopf").[1] But this was not the way he read the novel, nor the way he filmed it. On the contrary, the material dissimilarity between book and film could not have been more clearly highlighted.[2] With the many fades to white from film scenes to intertitles, he left what was written in the form of writing, with celluloid and the white screen momentarily acting as a substitute for paper. And he paid special attention to one aspect that cannot be conveyed visually, but which is nonetheless not excluded from reproduction in film: speech and the reporting of speech in narrative texts. This point was of primary importance to Döblin. In his view, writers needed to know the facts of life, by which he meant above all the various forms of everyday speech in their social and individual particularity. But merely registering these "voices of the city" was not enough—the writer must also be able to listen to his raw material in order to capture the significance of its social dimension.

Free Indirect Speech

In the 1920s, there was much listening to the inner workings of words and an interest in the relationship between the oral and how it was rendered in writing. This also drew attention to "free indirect speech" (FIS), an unspectacular device that has

1 He wrote: "It became clearer and clearer to me that a huge part of myself, of my behavior, my reactions, many things I had considered part of me, were nothing more than things described by Döblin in *Berlin Alexanderplatz*. Very simply, I had unconsciously turned Döblin's imaginings into my life. Yet once again it was the novel itself that helped me to overcome the alarming crisis that resulted and to work at establishing something that could eventually become, I hope, more or less the thing one calls an identity, to the extent that's even possible with all this screwed up mess." Fassbinder, "Cities of Humanity," 162.

2 In "Preliminary Remarks on *Querelle*" (1984), Fassbinder formulated the following demand for his version of filmed literature: "Always, at every stage, it must make clear that this is but one possible way of dealing with a work of art in another medium." In Töteberg and Lensing, *Anarchy of the Imagination*, 168.

been a staple of narrative texts since the mid-nineteenth century. It has been identified in the novels of Flaubert, Zola, and Dostoyevsky, in the work of Virginia Woolf, Thomas Mann, and James Joyce in the twentieth century, and occasionally in Döblin's *BA*. For example: "Eva's gentleman friend has gone to Brussels, and so she can invite Mieze to her place and show her all about how smart folks live."[3] Or, rather more complicated, this time with Reinhold as the character in question: "Suspiciously he fetched his landlady, the old procuress, and tried to sound her out: 'There was a big row in my place today, wasn't there?' It got that woman started off. He had done the right thing by Trude, she was a lazy pig, that one, she didn't even wanta iron her own petticoat. What, she wears petticoats; well, he never could stand for that, no, sir."[4]

The technical secret of FIS was quickly identified. Unlike in indirect speech, the sequence of the spoken sentence remains intact, although two shifts occur: the pronoun changes into the third person and the verb into the tense of the surrounding narrative, most often the imperfect. All of the other specific features—exclamations, peculiarities of syntax and dialect—are retained. As a result, spoken passages are shifted into an "unspeakable" sphere, blurring the line between narration and speech. Which is why FIS is "free" as well as "indirect," or, as Leo Spitzer put it at the time, this creates "the equivocal quality of this mode of expression, in turn lending it a sheen of mystery (now pseudo-objective, then pseudo-subjective, but always working with *pseudos*, with deceptions)."[5] Referring to

3 Alfred Döblin, *Berlin Alexanderplatz: The Story of Franz Biberkopf* (1929), trans. Eugene Jolas (London: Continuum, 2004), 225.

4 Ibid., 175.

5 Leo Spitzer, "Zur Entstehung der sog. 'erlebten Rede,'" *Germanisch-Romanische Monatsschrift* 16 (1928): 331.

Joyce's *Ulysses*, Roy Pascal notes that although FIS amplifies authenticity and immediacy, it also blurs the objectivity of the narrator.[6] At the beginning of the twentieth century, such effects were seen as a new quality, as evidence that antiauthoritarian and egalitarian tendencies had now advanced even into the structural details of literary narrative.

Cinema/"Poetry"

In the wake of this research, Pasolini also dealt repeatedly with FIS. In his essay "The Cinema of Poetry"—a lively blend of semiotic study and cultural critique—he attempted to use its features to explain structural conditions in film narratives.[7] First, he tries to distinguish between the sign systems of narrative text and cinema. While the former is "real, historically complex and mature," the latter is based on "nothing at all." Film images do not function like verbal language. They are not "abstract," being based instead on "pure and artificial abstraction" (167). As there are also no "dialects," the film author must constantly piece together his vocabulary. As a result, his work is "stylistic" (170) and thus "cannot be institutionalized" (177). This "language of reality" laid down in the film sequence, for which the filmmaker draws on visible reality, is best taken from a "patrimony of common signs" (167). These signs, which then form the basis of his filmic semantics, include the "primal language" of gestures that existed before spoken and written language, as well as visual imagery influenced by memory and dreams (168). If the film author were capable of working with this archaic

6 Roy Pascal, *The Dual Voice: Free Indirect Speech and Its Functioning in the Nineteenth-Century European Novel* (Manchester: Manchester University Press, 1977), 132.

7 Pier Paolo Pasolini, "The Cinema of Poetry" (1967), in *Heretical Empiricism*, trans. Louise K. Barnett and Ben Lawton (Washington, DC: New Academia Publishing, 2005), 167–86. Page numbers are given in parentheses following citations in the text.

material, of recognizing its ongoing effectiveness in the present, his works could reconnect with roots that are "extremely crude, almost animal-like" (168).

Because of this need to consciously select elements, then, the film image is fixated on "style." At the same time—due to "the expressive limitation imposed by the enormous size of the audience of film"—it must produce stereotypes of an "elementary conventional objectivity." This occasions the special "double nature" of film as both "extremely subjective and extremely objective" (173).

At this point, Pasolini brings FIS into play. In literature, he writes, its main function is to represent the verbal utterances of different social classes in their specific quality and render them usable in narrative (calling for an above-average "sociological" interest on the part of the author). Pasolini assumed that a construction equivalent to FIS also exists in film (176), and he called this construct "free indirect point-of-view" (FIPOV).

In cinema, FIPOV leads to very differentiated stylistic solutions and is even the prerequisite for the "cinema of poetry" of the essay's title (175). This type of cinema is characterized by certain sensibilities and the forced use of certain stylistic devices. In the sequence of film images, there is no equivalent for the reproduction of jargon, dialect, and everyday speech that enter narrative texts via FIS; nor for precise socially connoted perceptions—and if such equivalents do exist, then in Pasolini's view, movies have often enough proved their inability to gain access to them. In films with FIPOV markers, everything finally amounts to style, psychology, and expression, and Pasolini sees this as the real innovation of modern narrative cinema. He sees further hallmarks in plots that drift off into unconnected subunits and above all the conspicuous framing of shots.

The word "innovation" must be used cautiously here, as Pasolini sees all these attributes as so many deformations. The key quality of this stylistic approach is the "temptation to make another film." One perception is superimposed over another, so a second film hides behind the first. In this cinema, the author creates an essentially formalistic vision of the world, and FIPOV is the means of realizing a "technical language of poetry" (178). Such films are identifiable by their "obsessive shots and editing rhythms" (182), by their habit of "allowing the camera to be felt" (183).

In other words, wherever style takes control in this way, what FIPOV produces above all is pretext. Although the "bourgeois" filmmaker "lacking in class consciousness" poses as a representative of all humankind (174), he is in fact only interested in a particular kind of assertiveness. Consequently, he is capable of addressing nothing but his own "class interests" as his knowledge basically extends to one thing: "neurosis."

The fact that the social class in question takes the "neurotic" and his way of seeing as its center of interest is part of this assertiveness, articulated in updated form via FIPOV. Modern cinema of this kind always becomes especially nuanced where it revolves around nothing but the ego and its self-deceptions. To this end, the filmmaker takes his characters as mouthpieces, which is why they are so often drawn from the same social sphere. Moreover, Pasolini writes, "in the history of cinema, I would not be able to cite any cases of the total disappearance of the filmmaker into a character—at least until the early sixties" (177).

It is worth noting that by this point, Pasolini had long since left behind his attempt to systematize the semiotics of film, switching to a polemic on cultural politics. It is almost as if he is interested in this study of cinema's double articulation mainly as a way of delivering what he intended as a lethal blow to contemporary rivals like Bertolucci, Antonioni, Fellini, and Godard. For in the 1960s with their Marxist politicization, how was one to recover from the charge that one's artistic practice ultimately obeyed a late-capitalist logic, and that one's sophisticated exploration of subjectivities and "neuroses" via "formalisms" and self-critical "inner revolutions" did nothing more than help this neo-capitalism to "recover the ground lost in the battle with Marxism" (185).

However strident these accusations may sound, Pasolini's critique of European auteur cinema is not entirely unreasonable, especially where Antonioni is concerned. (And it could easily be applied to many of today's "auteur movies" as they cheerfully wallow once more in all manner of introspection, melancholy, and the hardships of family life—now doing so unmolested by in-depth criticism. [German Calamities (1980–2010)]) In spite of this, it is hard to understand what might have prompted Pasolini to lead the term "poetry" out onto the thin ice of such contradictory evaluations, where its composite quality could appear as both potentially beneficial and as a dubious distortion. Perhaps, speaking as a practitioner himself, he wished to keep options open for his own concept of an "other cinema" or an "other poetry" of the cinema. But it would have to be distinct from the other cinema of Godard, Antonioni, or Bertolucci. And this would be the case when "the original oneiric, barbaric, irregular, aggressive, visionary quality of cinema is found through its technical devices" (178).

There is no reason to see in this list of adjectives just another demonstration of Pasolini's traditionalism and yearning for forms of life and expression that had been rendered obsolete by "neo-capitalism." Instead, Pasolini outlined an aesthetic program in which his critique of the cinematic present was merely a negative point of departure for his own definition of a "technical language of poetry" for the cinema.

Against Representation

Long into the 1970s, any self-respecting intellectual was expected to analyze all manner of cultural and artistic materials in semiotic terms, understanding them as texts. In this light, Pasolini's remarks on a linguistics of film were of their time; but they were also a by-product of his erudition, as he possessed a keen knowledge of literature and literary theory. It was here that he came into contact with FIS and became alert to its implications. Applied to film, the result was as follows: However "unspeakable" FIS constructions may be when embedded in written text, they remain entirely transparent. But when transferred to a cinematographic context, they become barely intelligible. For apart from "feelable" cameras, what are such double articulations supposed to actually *look like* in a film? Like the distanced long shots with their handheld camera shake that are so characteristic of Pasolini's work?[8] One can see the FIS analogy as misguided or overstretched, but equally one can drop any call for practical relevance and simply accept its meaning in a "figurative" sense. Finally, one can credit Pasolini with a certain astuteness simply on the basis of his track record as an analyst of political matters and written utterances.[9]

Why this leniency all of a sudden? "The Cinema of Poetry" is not an academic text, so there is no reason to accuse it of a lack of theoretical consistency.[10] And after all, Pasolini did raise an interesting question that was rarely asked at the time—

8 In his treatment for a film about Saint Paul, Pasolini called for a FIS-like mixing of registers. In some cases, scenes were to be linked by *dissolvenza indirette*, indirect dissolves. The only thing that is clear about this instruction, however, is its incomprehensibility.

9 For example, in "From the Laboratory" (1965), his essay on Antonio Gramsci. On the basis of changing sentence structures and vocabulary in Gramsci's texts over time, Pasolini derived an entire novel of character development, not only in terms of political ideas, but also touching on early social and regional influences, including aspirations to social advancement.

the question of the social dimension lurking in the shadows of cinematographic "points of view."

The Subject as Ideologue, Speech as Material

The implications of FIS do not end here, however. In the late 1920s, Valentin Vološinov recapped the European debates surrounding FIS. In his book *Marxism and the Philosophy of Language*, some of the objections raised show similarities with Pasolini's later understanding of the matter, as they are based on similar premises. German turn-of-the-century linguists had traditionally shown great interest in FIS, and Vološinov acknowledged their sharp understanding of the inner tensions of such constructions. But from a Marxist viewpoint, such insight into the finer gradations of subjectivity was also highly suspect. His objections covered both the theoretical framework of FIS and its practical application. In both cases, he claimed, something was rendered absolute that should in fact be the subject of criticism, namely a view of "subjectivity" conceived of in terms of categories such as consciousness, style, imagination, empathy, taste, "mental fact."[11] His verdict on FIS: "It makes itself felt only as expression of an adventitious, subjective state. Typifying and individualizing coatings of the utterance have reached such an intense degree of differentiation in the linguistic consciousness that they have completely overshadowed and relativized an utterance's ideational core, the responsible social position imple-

10 Curiously, however, Pasolini's text did give rise to further attempts at codification, prompting Umberto Eco to publish a far more officious essay entitled "Articulations of the Cinematic Code" (1970), in which he reprimanded Pasolini for his use of terms such as "mimesis" or "semiology of reality." In *Movies and Methods: An Anthology*, ed. Bill Nichols, vol. 1 (Berkeley: University of California Press, 1976), 590–604.

11 This corresponds to Pasolini's criticism of the auteur films of his time and his ambivalent assessment of FIS, forty years later, with no knowledge of Vološinov's text, but on the basis of common political and theoretical assumptions.

mented in it. The utterance has virtually ceased to be an object for serious ideational consideration."[12]

A more responsible social position and the serious ideational consideration of utterances would then consist in a view of subjectivity conceived of in less arbitrary, not quite so individualized terms. For, "the inner subjective personality with its own self-awareness does not exist as a material fact, usable as a basis for causal explanation, but it exists as an ideologeme. [...] Language lights up the inner personality and its consciousness; language creates them and endows them with intricacy and profundity—and it does not work the other way. [...] Consequently, a word is not an expression of inner personality; rather, inner personality is an expressed or inwardly impelled word. And the word is an expression of social intercourse, of the social interaction of material personalities."[13]

What in the German context with its idealistic leanings had been treated as a purely aesthetic and epistemological problem (person/figure as owner of an inner life; question of the scope of grammatical determinability; ratio and relation of narrator/character and "objective"/"subjective") was approached in the Soviet Union on the basis of a semiotic approach and thus of an opposing conception of the subject: rather than being creations of consciousness, thoughts are reflexes triggered by material forms of intercourse. Consequently, consciousness is always false, as the truth of its own utterances eludes it—as does the structure of the economic conditions by which it is brought forth.

Mikhail Bakhtin (who is presumed to have used Vološinov as a pseudonym) never tired of viewing the subject as the effect

12 Valentin N. Vološinov, *Marxism and the Philosophy of Language* (1929), trans. Ladislav Matejka and I. R. Titunik (Cambridge, MA: Harvard University Press, 1986), 158.

13 Ibid., 152–53.

of semiotic processes most fittingly portrayed in the relational principle of the "dialogical": an utterance is never neutral, rather it always refers to a specific context. The word is a hinge joining levels that overlap but that do not fully coincide. Dialogue can denote the conversational to and fro between figures in physical proximity, but in narrative texts it also takes place between words, their meanings and connotations, between statement and enunciation, between narrator, characters, books, and the reader.

Biberkopf as Ideologue

As well as calling the narrative text itself into question, Russian semiotics also accorded it a privileged role in illustrating and shaping this dialogical dimension. Only here, in the narrative structures, networks of "voices," and levels of narrative, can the ambivalences of language production be acted out in a way to which neither everyday speech nor academic writing has access (because they tend toward a monological form of expression).

In this context, Bakhtin returned again and again to the novels of Dostoyevsky. At one point, he describes Dostoyevsky's method as follows: "Not a single element of the work is structured from the point of view of a nonparticipating 'third person.'"[14] To substantiate this claim, it suffices to read a few pages of *Crime and Punishment*. While planning a murder, and in order to spare himself unpleasant surprises, Raskolnikov intends to think through all of the possible options and consequences. As his thoughts go back and forth, however, the voice of another entity is heard that could be called his conscience or, in Freudian terms, his superego. Here, too, its modus operandi is to reassure, threaten, and censor at the same time, making

14 Mikhail Bakhtin, *Problems of Dostoyevsky's Poetics* (1929), trans. and ed. Caryl Emerson (Minneapolis: University of Minnesota Press, 1984), 18.

contradictory demands on the subject concerning even the most rational considerations.

It was narrative conditions such as these that prompted the following claim from Vološinov: in the word, he writes, "I give myself verbal shape from another's point of view, ultimately from the point of view of the community to which I belong."[15] Even when thinking, one is never alone; even a conversation with oneself, inner monologue, or stream of consciousness always already includes an interlocutor. Which is also why there is no need for "a single element of the work [to be] structured from the point of view of a nonparticipating 'third person,'" since such third parties are always already present in every thought process anyway.

Perhaps it is now clearer what this early brand of semiotics that developed in the late 1920s in the Soviet Union might have to do with Döblin's novel or Fassbinder's film. The figure of Franz Biberkopf is synthesized along similar lines. Though sparsely described and held together by little more than his name,[16] on another level he is far more lavishly endowed: Biberkopf is extremely talkative.

He speaks a great deal, constantly pondering things and conversing with others. What he says always bears traces of what others have been saying: the official announcements of the day, all the various "voices of the city." As a result, this figure, clearly defined on the one hand as subproletarian, is less clearly defined on the other since his diverging wishes, attitudes, and opinions also appear as responses to pleas and appeals. This creates a muddle of the most contradictory character traits. Biberkopf is

15 Vološinov, *Marxism and the Philosophy of Language*, 86.

16 As described by Döblin in the novel, Biberkopf was "fat," a "tall, big-boned fellow," "weighing almost two hundredweights," "five foot ten," with a "full face" and "lively eyes" "that are brown." That's about all.

a semi-idiot, but clever; foolish, but wise; good-natured and malicious; aggressive, cynical, and yielding; opinionated and fickle, gregarious and solitary, smug and dissatisfied, sadistic and masochistic, heterosexual and "homophile." Things are no better with regard to his political views: he has a communist past, shares socialist ideas, but could also be or become a Nazi.

Biberkopf himself is thus a montage both as a character and on the level of his speech acts.

Oh Dear, Oh Well, Uh-Oh

Fassbinder identified this constructed quality and took it into account, modifying it via his own understanding of language. While the material supplied by Döblin (sayings, clichés, jokes) would have allowed him to draw on a fascinating archive of linguistic remnants and curios, he chose to replace the typical Berlin slang that is everywhere in the book with a range of dialects and speech patterns from southern Germany, East Prussia, and the Rhineland. But his attention focused above all on phenomena of language that are usually credited with the least meaning. Even in the most conventional figures of speech, he saw a kind of exchange, despite or because of their "ideological" connotations. ("A man needs what a man needs, simple as that." "How right you are, Mr. Biberkopf, I couldn't agree more.") Further examples of Fassbinder's attentiveness to all things verbal are easily found. One striking feature is a recurring form of dialogue that has no equivalent in Döblin's work: in replies, parts of the previous utterance are picked up, doubled, and repeated. (Biberkopf: "It depends on the earnings." Pums: "You're right. You are quite right there. It depends on the earnings. That's exactly what I say.") Although this might be seen as a way of underlining the alleged emptiness of such interpersonal communication, it actually confirms that the act of speaking is capable of producing meaning even when the words themselves are all but meaningless.

In *BA*/3 there is a scene in which Fassbinder takes this to extreme lengths. While thinking about new ways to earn money, Lina remembers her "Uncle" Lüders. Although out of work, he goes door to door selling shoelaces. Lina makes the connection and the result is an exchange between the three characters during which the word "shoelaces" goes back and forth a dozen times.[17] These shoelaces convey no information of any kind, they contribute nothing to the plot, and one "shoelaces" more or less really would make no difference. Nonetheless, this to and fro is not only in accordance with the notion of enunciation in discourse theory, it also acts as a practical demonstration of that theory.[18] In this sequence, Fassbinder shows with great clarity that ties can be established between people even by tautological speech acts. Even if it is always the same word that does the rounds here, it is never the same utterance. At every turn, it changes as a result of intonations, gestures, and facial expressions: the pleasure of inspiration, tension resolved due to new hope. (In addition, a discrete new element is added to a list of key signifiers running through *BA*: arm, hand, leg, foot, and shoe.)

On occasion, this function of speech is reflected on by the characters themselves. In *BA*/5, the landlord asks Biberkopf what he wants to drink. "A beer and a schnapps." To which the barman replies, "You see, I could have told you that myself. Why

17 And because this dialogue is so charming, here it is in full: Lüders: "And shoelaces are something people always need." Lina: "Shoelaces. What do you say to that? Shoelaces!" Franz: "Well, what should I say? Shoelaces!" Lina: "Shoelaces." Lüders: "Right, shoelaces." Lina: "Listen, just asking, about the shoelaces, I mean. Do you think one could do something, for Franz—with shoelaces?" Lüders: "Why not. Shoelaces always sell. One more or less won't make any difference." Lina: "Shoelaces. Franz, come on, be happy." Franz: "Yeah, I get the message. Shoelaces. OK, I'm happy as well." Lina: "Shoelaces. Why didn't I think of that myself? I knew Uncle Lüders could help us. I knew it all along." Franz: "You knew it all along, that's right." (*They lift their bottles of beer.*) Lüders: "Cheers." Franz: "Cheers." This scene is not in the novel.

bother asking if you already know just what the other person's going to say anyway?" In *BA*/13, the now one-armed Biberkopf tries to bandage Meck's hand, burned during a burglary. Biberkopf: "It's idiotic that this had to happen today." Meck: "You can't choose your defeats." Biberkopf: "So they say, and it's probably true, but that doesn't say anything really." And when Meck tries to help: "No, no. I have to do that on my own. Bandaging like that, you know, calls for sensitivity from the person applying it, and from the one who feels it. Sometimes, I notice while I'm speaking that what I'm saying is a load of baloney, but I like to say it anyway." (The tension in this intimate scene is heightened by the fact that Meck knows something that the other doesn't: Mieze, Biberkopf's girlfriend, has been murdered.)

As well as speech that establishes contact in this way, there is another kind that deliberately obstructs or avoids such contacts. This applies to a type of communication practiced throughout *BA* by Reinhold: fussy expressions of displeasure and the use of language in manipulative ways (like in a bad movie script).

18 It is hard not to think here of definitions of "enunciation" by Derrida and others. Foucault: "A statement exists outside any possibility of reappearing [...] and if in these conditions an identical formulation reappears, with the same words, [...] in fact exactly the same sentence, it is not necessarily the same statement." Michel Foucault, *Archaeology of Knowledge*, trans. A. M. Sheridan Smith (London: Routledge, 2002), 100–1. Or Lacan: "You can see clearly then that this is the concrete discourse of the individual subject, of the person who speaks and who makes himself understood. It is the discourse that can be recorded on a record. The other is what all of that includes as a possibility of decomposition, of reinterpretation, of resonance, of metaphorical or metonymical effects." Jacques Lacan, *The Seminar of Jacques Lacan V: The Formations of the Unconscious*, trans. Cormac Gallagher (London: Karnac Books, 2002), 7. In the realm of film theory, by contrast, Christian Metz tried in his book on "the impersonal enunciation" to apply Émile Benveniste's distinction between utterance and enunciation (*énoncé* and *énonciation*) to film. Although he believed his approach based on "impersonality" to be at one with the then current and perhaps binding standards in subject and discourse theory, it was in fact based on their distortion. Metz attributed qualities to (filmic) enunciations that for Benveniste

And because in certain cases this could be mistaken for the inauthentic mode of speech known as irony, there is a dialogue setting this right. In *BA*/12, Reinhold uses a pretext to lure Mieze to an out-of-town resort where he plans to make a move on her. In the first phase of their conversation, the tone is extravagant. Reinhold: "Just tell us what you'd like to talk about, Miss Mieze. I for one am quite fond of a little chat now and then." Mieze: "Oh, I don't mind. You talk and talk, but what you talk about doesn't really matter. The main thing is you're happy and enjoy life." Mieze again, shortly after: "Do you really have to resort to such stupid tricks, Mr. Reinhold?" Reinhold: "You never know in advance whether you'll need tricks or not. Usually they're necessary. Sometimes, thank God, they're not. And that's how I prefer it. I far prefer that, Miss Mieze." Mieze: "With me, Mr. Reinhold, you don't need any tricks. You can talk straight with me. Do you understand? With me you can, if you know how, talk straight."

In the same register, opinions and declarations are also used throughout as a form of blockade. In a barroom conversation, one man says, "An enormous amount of capital is squandered

were specifically typical of (verbal) utterances (unspecific, impersonal, tied to the third person). Moreover, he associates the speech act in film only to the most conventional "reflexive" elements in films (mirrors, windows, voice-overs, looking into the camera, nested framing elements). By way of conclusion, he states that every shot is "to a certain extent" a deictic "this one." Spread so generously across the entire field of possible audiovisual phenomena, and relying on nothing but the fragile concept of "enunciation," his theorizing amounted to a practical nothing in terms of definition: in films, "it" speaks everywhere; the film utterance "always says the same thing: 'this is a film.'" In this way, a formal approach that might be suited to addressing the wealth of material and diversity of registers encompassed by film in all their specificity was transformed into a theory for everything and for nothing, and into another example of what might be called "cinephilia" acting theoretically. Christian Metz, *L'énonciation impersonelle ou le site du film* (Paris: Meridiens Klincksieck, 1991). A shorter piece with the same title has appeared in English: Christian Metz, Béatrice Durand-Sendrail, and Kristen Brookes, "The Impersonal Enunciation, or the Site of Film," *New Literary History* 22, no. 3 (Summer 1991).

in the world. In America, they even let the wheat rot; whole crops. Did you know that?" Bruno: "Sure. Everyone knows that. It's even crazier in Australia. They have prehistoric lizards, outlandishly long. They live in swampy, murky pools. No one knows what they live from. No one!" (*BA*/5).

In *BA*/2, a significant revaluation takes place. Biberkopf meets some old acquaintances from his time as a communist. Since he is now selling the Nazi-affiliated *Völkischer Beobachter* newspaper, they would really like to give him a "proletarian hiding." This doesn't happen; the tension subsides, and Biberkopf is able to leave the bar unscathed. Whereupon Dreske, by far the eldest in the group, speaks directly into the camera as it moves in toward him: "Let the despicable, renegade scoundrels, encouraged by the bourgeoisie and social chauvinists, disparage the constitution of the Soviets! It simply accelerates and deepens the rift between the revolutionary workers of Europe and the supporters of Scheidemann and so on. The oppressed masses are on our side."

As a piece of agitation, this text could not be more orthodox or monotonous. It is immune to objections and rendered meaningless by frequent repetition—and in the novel, it really is no more than that. In Fassbinder's film, the actor's delivery alters it completely. Soft, quiet, and slowed down, spoken with a southern German drawl that makes a soft, good-natured impression, the text is charged with considerable melancholy. In this portrayal, it is relieved of a function that it no longer possesses anyway, as no one now believes it capable of achieving anything. In this way, Fassbinder introduces a knowledge of later developments: this type of statement will have become obsolete, the proletariat will not be victorious, it will even have ceased to be relevant as a social force and as a historical subject. (Nevertheless, the device also hints at the existence of the communist Left in Germany, before and after 1933, after 1945, in the GDR, its delegitimization in West Germany—and, one might add, up to the present.)

Fassbinder's *BA* offers many other chances to observe Döblin's idea of "authentic" speech. For Döblin, "true" speech involves an exchange that transforms speaker and listener, and this is reflected in the first minutes of the first episode of the series. Just out of prison, confused by the impressions of the city, working himself up into a state by singing chauvinistic songs, Biberkopf is picked up and taken in by an Eastern European rabbi. At his home, Nachum tells the story of the rise and abrupt fall of Zannovich. In this scene, the rabbi draws Biberkopf out of his catatonic state into speech. ("He doesn't talk. … You see, a man tells stories and talks with another man, time passes better that way.") Here, then, the function of narrative is already defined as nourishment, therapy, and counseling. ("There's a lot on Earth, a man could tell a lot of stories about it, when he's young and when he's old"; "Don't worry about yourself so much! Listen to others! Who says you're so important?") [19]

In *BA*/7 the homosexual Willy demonstrates a positively Adamic act of naming, although in this case it is merely intended to justify theft: "And what's this? … Sure, it's a watch. It's not a boot and not a canary, but if you like, you can call it a boot, as you wish. That's your business."

As well as dialogues between characters, Döblin (and Fassbinder followed him in this) also gave a dialogical quality to individual parts of a conversation, causing the speakers to inwardly become montages. Biberkopf is offended and refuses to speak to Mieze. She: "Come on! Say something! Anything!" He: "Silent night, holy night; all is calm, all is bright. I am small, my heart is pure. Siegesmund can't help it if he's handsome. Siegesmund can't help it if he's loved. From heaven high I hail,

19 The story of Zannovich is also a parable of failed Jewish integration in Europe.

and bring you a new tale." Her: "That's mean. That's so mean!" (*BA*/12).

But there are also opportunities to let what there is to say and think directly be said and thought directly. There are enough reasons to be outraged, to despair, or to wish or call for change. In a bar scene in *BA*/10, Biberkopf meets a carpenter who has been driven out of his flat by the misery of everyday life and who launches into a long, touching lament about the welfare state, even if the bar's owner doesn't like to hear such talk.

The carpenter: "I don't need Marxism either, or anything else like that. What I do need I can count on my fingers every day. When someone beats the hell out of me, I know what it means! … And if I've got kids, and the oldest one is bowlegged from rickets, I can't send her away somewhere. Maybe the school will send her to the country; but only maybe. The worst thing is the kids learn only as much as we did. Just imagine: only as much as we did. They don't teach them anything we didn't learn. How can anything ever change? … And if I have to go to the doctor with rheumatism, there are thirty of us sitting in the waiting room. Then the doctor says to me: 'You had the rheumatism already, right?' … He just doesn't believe me. So then I'm sent to a medical examiner. If you want to be sent somewhere by the state insurance, they always dock your wages for it. You'd have to arrive with your head under your arm before they'd send you for free. … Poverty should be for those who want it. Let the others be poor, for all I care. Just count me out! In the end, you can't stand it anymore, when it's always the same people who are poor."

Biberkopf then leaves the bar and continues mulling over what he has just heard in a different register—that of a mumbled interior monologue. His speech reacts to another speech, splicing its components together with other "ideologemes": "Rumbledly tumbledy dumbledy dee. Wait, just wait a little while, Haarmann, the murderer, will come to you with a hatchet and a smile, to make liver sausage out of you. He still doesn't believe me. I have to go to a medical examiner. If I want the insurance to send me somewhere, they always dock money for it. You'd have to arrive with your head under your arm before they'd send you somewhere. Wait, just wait a little while. … Her uterus has become joined with her rectum. They operated on her, but it didn't help internally. … And the kids learn exactly the same as we did. You can imagine what comes of that. Drink, drink, brother mine, drink! Leave all your cares behind! Drink, drink, brother mine, drink! And with a nervous illness, you're perfectly fit. Anyone with a nervous illness is perfectly healthy. And nobody needs Karl Marx for that anymore. But it's true nevertheless. Forget all your worries, forget all your pain, and life will be merry again. What does a bowlegged person do in the country?"

Poor Folk

In his first novel *Poor Folk*, Dostoyevsky also raises questions concerning realism and representation, portrayal and illustration. The main character Makar Devushkin is indignant about Gogol's *The Overcoat*. He feels patronized, ridiculed as a petit bourgeois by the story, and parodied by its picturesque details: "One hides oneself sometimes, one hides oneself, one tries to conceal one's weak points, one's afraid to show one's nose at times anywhere because one is afraid of tittle-tattle, because they can work up a tale against you about anything in the world—anything. And here now all one's private and public life is being dragged into literature, it is all printed, read, laughed and gossiped about!" [20]

This discontent, formulated around 1844, is only too understandable. Examples of similar misrepresentations are still

20 Quoted from Bakhtin, *Problems of Dostoyevsky's Poetics*, 58.

plentiful today, not least in films, although, as far as I can see, they are rarely complained about by those affected.[21]

Could this be done differently? Pasolini once made fun of the idea, proposed by Bertolucci or Antonioni, of dignifying characters from the lower classes by putting lines from a sophisticated literary repertoire in their mouths.[22] Another question is possible here: Can there be a society of people who mutually acknowledge each other as equals? Does one group really speak to the other, are they capable of truly acknowledging each other, and if they can, how do they perceive each other? Just assuming that Pasolini's notion of inserting one point of view into another were to correspond to everyday modes of perception (which it doesn't) then it would also be necessary to take into account the ways people judge each other from their various social, cultural, and economic positions, also determined by age and gender. Taking indifference and death wish as opposite extremes, one can identify at least the following intervening degrees of involvement: contempt, disgust, condescension, pity, boredom, ingratiation, envy, sexual attraction, inhibition, shame, pride, defiance. (In this context, love would be the special case of a potential transgression in all directions.)

A cinematic realization of such conditions is hard to imagine because it so rarely occurs. This must be put down to media-specific crudeness, an instrumental populism where social differ-

21 At least where economic and class-related inequalities are concerned. By contrast, especially in Anglo-American film and television productions since the early 1990s, questions of race, sexuality, ethnicity, and to an extent also religion have come to the fore. As a consequence, it is possible to complain or, often enough, joke about inadequate representations. [Jewish Matters: Representation]

22 While Bertolucci bitched back, "Antonioni makes films about ashtrays. [...] Pasolini is so decadent in real life that he tries to cover it up by making his films austere." Quoted in Bob Colacello, *Holy Terror: Andy Warhol Close Up* (New York: HarperCollins, 1990), 36–37.

ences tend to be either blurred or overdrawn.[23] Another aspect of this crudeness is the demonstrative focus of a large section of cinema productions on the juste-milieu and its values (achievement, property, freedom of contract, initiative, responsibility for and control over one's own actions and one's own life.)[24] This centrism is especially striking in the United States, although it is fueled there by a belief in the necessity of "being oneself," the fundamental possibility of acquiring an equal share, and the potential for resolving any conflict by outstanding personal commitment, which is not the case in German films. This is also why "representations" in German films appear so much more monotonous and oppressive, regardless of whether this is down to benevolence, cynicism, or dull scriptwriting. The "solidarity with the weak" that is so often evoked in Germany nonetheless mostly takes the form of a trite, very general orientation toward the misery of the world. This "politics of

23 "Social" realism has certainly had its great moments, but for such moments to happen, there must be "playing fields," economic frameworks, industrial or political niches. Examples include the proletarian films of the 1920s, the New Deal films of the 1930s, the worker films produced by WDR television in 1970s West Germany, part of the German New Wave, and since the 1990s certain material produced by cable TV channels in the United States. Hundreds of films from East Germany's state film production organization DEFA also set standards here: in the GDR, the film production of an entire country was obliged to create narratives that dramatize the relationship of the individual to the institutions of society and the process by which an individual becomes a proper member of a community. One of the great exceptions of the past decade was the widely praised American series *The Wire* (2002–08). As well as being an updated version of the large-scale realist novel of the nineteenth century, it was also an example of journalism and social democracy in the best sense. But this is not the kind of realism I am referring to here.

24 Fassbinder painted many caustic portraits of this "class." An excellent example is to be found in *BA*/6. The couple who have just run Biberkopf over with their car are torn between duty, pity, and the protection of their own interests. The woman takes a pragmatic view and says they should flee the scene ("It's his own fault"). I would also like to mention the scene of ostentatious noncontact between the imaginary historical and bourgeois contemporary figures in Godard's *Weekend* (1967), in which the petit bourgeoisie are portrayed as thoroughly dissatisfied, obnoxious, impertinent, and ignorant.

the heart" is then often affirmed by film reviewers who describe a meeting of equals on a level playing field even in cases of blatant social exploitation. Together with the related phenomenon of "keeping a respectful distance," this "level playing field" has become a widespread euphemism for a mode of speaking about others that would not dream of devoting anything other than a sharp, curious gaze to these weak people, and which does not assume itself to be implicated in this spectacle of misery. [German Calamities (1980–2010)]

However you look at it, social differences and interlocking perspectives have been and continue to be portrayed more often and more incisively in literature than in film, with some of the best examples to be found in the work of Marcel Proust. One passage can illustrate this as well as any other, so here is the second scene at the Verdurins' salon in *Swann's Way*: the primary social contrast is between the haute bourgeoisie and the aristocracy. To be precise, as elites can themselves be subdivided into endless substrata, one "low society" is actually contrasted with two "high" ones. The Verdurins represent the lower level, and their entourage, all pillars of society, is described in exclusively negative terms. Everything about them is ridiculous: their narrow territorialism, their presumptuous judgments, their feeble wordplay, and their crude familiarity.

The highest levels of society are represented by Swann and Forcheville. The Verdurins know precious little about either of them, but they think Swann a snob, not seeing his reserve as the expression of kindness and respect that it is. Forcheville, on the other hand, is so modest of appearance, so flexible in his manners, that he arouses no suspicion. Unlike Swann, who, as someone with a "Jewish" background, is not part of the aristocracy but is very welcome among its members, Forcheville belongs to its upper echelons, although Swann is the only person in the Verdurins' world who knows this.

The scene is set in motion by Odette, a "kept" woman. She is the focus of Swann and Forcheville's interest. One wants her, the other has her, and both only frequent the Verdurins on her account. But Swann, who has ample reason to look down on this circle, does not do so, as his love also embraces the "little clan" and even their foolish attitudes. He socializes below his rank, but he rarely notices this, whereas Forcheville clearly identifies the narrow-mindedness of this milieu and occasionally makes disparaging remarks. He is the snob that Swann is taken for.

In this tangle of overlapping opinions and misjudgments, Forcheville and the narrator Marcel are the ones in command. The privilege of describing the characters is reserved for the narrator himself, giving him access to the considerable comic potential of the scene and its "objectivity." Or at least that is how it appears when viewed in isolation. For what on the one hand seems funny or sad becomes, over the course of the novel, a central element: forbearance or blindness caused by love. False assumptions have consequences, too. Everyone is dependent on everyone else, and in the long term we see the demise of "high" society as it mixes with the "low," leading in turn to the rise of the Verdurins—a transformation of social structures ultimately brought about by sexual or matrimonial exchanges and a shifting of cultural parameters.

Not that this scene or Proust's concept of the novel is in any way comparable with *BA*. What they do have in common is never, at any point, to have assumed that "simple people" live simple lives or have a more direct connection to some kind of unmediated experience.

Since the social framework of *BA* embraces only an underclass, however, the tone adopted cannot always be distinguished from the "popular tone" that Adorno found so tasteless and odious in a certain type of German literature (and in *BA*, even Death speaks Berlin slang). But Döblin's social perspective is not based on a realism of misery or the calculated attribution of picturesque qualities. To suspect *BA*'s demotic intentions (*Volkstümlichkeit*) of any link with an ethno-nationalistic agenda (*das Völkische*) would be to miss the point that this demotic quality was of fundamental importance to Döblin and Fassbinder. In both cases, it is based on an assumption of generalization that is irreconcilable with "representation" and social stereotypes.[25] Biberkopf is not a "representative" of any class or social position. His status is precarious in more than just an economic sense: just as one can say of the unconscious that everybody has one, everyone is not as free as they think they are, and no one knows what it is that structures what they say and do. In other words, the place where *BA* unfolds is shaped by a realm that is "lowly" in more than just social terms.

Echoes of Archaic States

Döblin made very different demands on his work as a novelist. On the one hand: immediacy, being of the present, modern world, current use of language, journalistic interest in the issues of the day, addressing the reader without "literary" fuss. On the other: psychoanalysis, the primordial, tragedy and the question of being (Berlin as "the Whore of Babylon," Biberkopf as Isaac, Job, Jesus). The one level was meant to update the other, which in turn added undercurrents to the former.

In the 1920s, the tendency toward the "mythical" and the legend, toward being and all things elementary, was widespread, and it was not incompatible with Marxist thinking. It thus formed a level where revolutionaries from the Left and the Right

25 Döblin on the sociological dimension of his book: "I am interested in characters who cannot simply attach themselves to a specific class, in the 'problem of people who stand between the classes.'" This comment is from a newspaper clipping included with no further details in Prangel, *Materialien zu "Berlin Alexanderplatz"*, 41.

could meet. In the context of artistic production, this also represented an attempt to elaborate a post- or non-bourgeois concept of realism, to withdraw from unproductive affiliations (rationality, psychology, "inner life," "diagnosing the present"), thus aiming for a multidimensional portrayal of reality.

The same intention was attributed by Bakhtin to his study of the "carnivalesque" and its close relative, the Menippean satire. In his book on Dostoyevsky, he gives it the following characteristics: rather than a genre, it is a cultural technique; its influence runs across historical periods, emerging at isolated points and not restricted by nationality, media, or genre. In Bakhtin's version, these features read like a list of modernist techniques and approaches: resistance to the legitimacy of high culture, preference for stark contrasts, arbitrary text insertions, absurd ideas, input from current events, and the casual mixing of various genres.[26] (His points of reference are the romances of antiquity, the Socratic dialogues, the novels of Petronius, Dante, Rabelais, Cervantes, Swift, Sterne.) On the Menippean stage, the social, economic, and "intellectual" status quo is turned upside down, gender and social class become interchangeable, inequality based on age is abolished, and all forms of presumption are brought down. These altered values take the human body as their object. It is desecrated, its insides turned outward, its parts and orifices occupied by primal impulses. Bakhtin had already found examples of this drastic and sometimes horrifying "laying bare" in the work of Dostoyevsky: "At the heart of the genre lies the discovery of the inner man—'one's own self,' accessible not to passive self-observation but only through an active dialogic approach to one's own self, destroying that naïve wholeness of one's notions about the self that lies at the heart off the lyric, epic, and tragic image of man. A dialogic approach

26 Bakhtin, *Problems of Dostoyevsky's Poetics*, 114–22.

to oneself breaks down the outer shell of the self's image, that shell which exists for other people, determining the external assessment of a person (in the eyes of others) and dimming the purity of self-consciousness."[27]

One cannot say that movies have a special affinity with this approach. Where links do exist, they are more common in genre films than in auteur cinema. Exceptions include the films of Hitchcock, Buñuel, Fellini, Bergman, Glauber Rocha, the Surrealists and their American offshoots (Kenneth Anger), as well as the films of Jack Smith and some by Andy Warhol. (Also in various types of horror and splatter movies and probably even in the starkness of much pornography, in both cases before their ironic turn.) West German cinema of the 1970s also made a major contribution here in the form of Herbert Achternbusch, Rosa von Praunheim, and Werner Schroeter. And, of course, the list must also include Pasolini.[28]

Fassbinder, too, displayed such affinities in many works, but in *BA* he was tied into this sphere by Döblin. And the action really is merry and holy, vulgar and devastating, all at the same time. Biberkopf's "grotesque" body is subjected to violence that shakes the bones and pierces the heart. (Döblin's inclination toward portrayals of extreme violence was often held against him and described as bloodthirstiness, cheap shock tactics, and artistic weakness.) It may be appropriate here to quote what Deleuze wrote about Pasolini's films: "A poetic consciousness, which is not strictly aestheticist or technicist, but rather mystical or 'sacred'. This allows Pasolini to bring the perception-image, or the neurosis of his characters, on to a level of vulgarity and

27 Ibid., 120.

28 His choice of source material put him in especially direct contact with this sphere: Geoffrey Chaucer's *The Canterbury Tales*, Giovanni Boccaccio's *Decameron*, the stories of Medea and Oedipus, the Gospels of Matthew and Paul, and Sade's *The 120 Days of Sodom*.

bestiality in the lowest subject matter, while reflecting them in a pure poetic consciousness animated by the mythical or sacralizing element. It is this permutation of the trivial and the noble, this communication between the excremental and the beautiful, this projection onto myth, which Pasolini had already diagnosed in free indirect discourse as the essential form of literature."[29] Fassbinder wrote something similar about *BA*: "This work of art [...] helps you accept the ordinary as the real thing, as sacred, without itself being ordinary or sacred, or making much of itself as an account of the real thing, and all this without being cruel, something literary works as significant as this one often are."[30]

But when transposing the action provided by Döblin, Fassbinder also scaled it to the conditions of the audiovisual medium. Which is also why the "pornography" of *BA* takes place largely in the field of oral pleasures, with the mouth acting simultaneously as a tool for speaking, biting, and sucking. At moments of extreme dread, Lamprecht's face opens up into a gaping hole, resembling an ancient Greek theater mask, emitting a silent scream.[31]

For Fassbinder, drawing the consequences from Döblin's novel also meant abandoning himself unreservedly to the apocalyptic mystery play, accepting its premises and inner requirements—not just referring to the basic facts of life, but also acting them out. In this way, Fassbinder brought Döblin's text, with its tendency toward stodginess, thoroughly into its own.

So what was it that made such mythicizing so attractive to a left-wing artistic intelligentsia (if only among its most far-

29 Deleuze, *Cinema 1*, 75.

30 Fassbinder, "Cities of Humanity," 161.

31 A similar approach was taken by Andy Warhol in his poster design for *Querelle*: one undressed man stands behind another, his tongue stuck far out, touching the other man's ear.

sighted and undogmatic members)? What part could it play within a Marxist view? What does it mean for Pasolini "to bring the neurosis of his characters to a level of vulgarity and bestiality" or to see the "oneiric," "barbaric," and "aggressive" as necessary qualities of artistic production? And necessary for what?

The last question is more or less rhetorical, as an answer is contained in what precedes it. Another answer takes us in the following direction: It is not enough to adopt a social perspective for its own sake, and the social should not be approached in terms of the misery of the world. Reality cannot be captured purely from the material side or via the mimicry of total actuality. To "narrate" reality in a more fundamental way, it is necessary to create a space of diversity that tries to avoid forms of distancing such as proxy figures, mere generality, and false identity. This calls for a sustaining symbolism within whose mediated immediacy or indirect freedom one can then visualize the violence of conditions that would otherwise be hard to portray.

Myths, too, narrate and give figurative form to things taking place beyond the reach of sight and insight on a macroeconomic level. The image of the dismembered body raised the issue of the subject before psychoanalysis formalized its conditions as knowledge. For Thomas Mann, the structural similarities between a psychoanalytical and a mythical economy were obvious. In his speech celebrating Freud's eightieth birthday, he spoke of this using an apposite image:

> The feast is the abrogation of time, an event, a solemn narrative being played out conformably to an immemorial pattern; the events in it take place not for the first time, but ceremonially according to the prototype. It achieves presentness as feasts do, recurring in time. [...] In antiquity each feast was essentially a dramatic performance, a mask; it was the scenic reproduction, with priests as actors, of

> stories about the gods. [...] The Christian Middle Ages had their mystery play [...] their carnival farce. [...] The artist eye has a mythical slant upon life, which makes it look like a farce, like a theatrical performance of a prescribed feast, like a Punch and Judy epic.

Such a performance also demands "that this mythical slant pass over and become subjective in the performers themselves, become a festival and mythical consciousness of part and play, for an epic to be produced."[32]

Now what is the subject of these festive and sometimes merry performances? Suffering, dying, and rising up (like Jesus). With each repetition, the things that are most irksome and unacceptable to the rational mind are performed and made present in dramatic action.[33]

In Döblin's work, archaicization and proletarianization included a psychoanalytical dimension that is absent, for example, in Brecht's work. Although in the revised version of his play *The Decision* (1930), he added a motif that amounts to the same thing: the mask. In the play, the mask marks the difference between the revolutionary proletarian and the revolutionary of the heart with his longing for spontaneous action.[34] At the start, all of the characters are masked, before the accused tears his off. This reveals him as the "human" that, as a "revolutionary," he should have worked to overcome. With this act, Brecht tells us, he merely becomes once more what he had never stopped being in the first place.

32 Thomas Mann, "Freud and the Future," *Saturday Review of Literature*, July 25, 1936; in Thomas Mann, *Death in Venice, Tonio Kröger and Other Writings*, ed. Frederick A. Lubich (New York: Continuum, 1999), 293–94.

33 Alongside its many charms, the most striking characteristic of postwar socialist cinema is the "abolition of death."

At a given time, a new technology may be better and more effective than an old one. At the end of the 1970s, there was an opportunity to create what Pasolini called the "visionary" or "oneiric" in the medium with the broadest reach, as a cinema or television of cruelty. But successfully coaxing this cruelty (and subtlety) out of film or television could not be due to any reliance on an audiovisual presentation. On the contrary, they had to be coaxed out of a medium that normally maintains close links with illusions and common denominators, and that would always prefer to broadcast only "what everyone already knows anyway." For Fassbinder, however, this deeply illusionary quality was also the basis for his own forms of beauty, as well as allowing him to make something that was highly sophisticated but without arrogance, emotional without being overwhelming, and fashionable without being inane. Fassbinder wanted to be "of the people," but in analytical, sensitive, and historically specific ways.[35]

34 The young comrade says, "I shall do the simple human thing. [...] My heart beats for the revolution. [...] I am for freedom." The three agitators: "Be quiet! You'll betray us!" Bertolt Brecht, *The Decision*, trans. John Willett, in *Collected Plays*, ed. John Willett, vol. 3 (London: Methuen, 1997), 84.

35 In his last film *Salò, or the 120 Days of Sodom* (1975), Pasolini made a significant disavowal, withdrawing the positive charge from the feast of carnal splendor and the satirical and "utopian" Menippean tradition, emaciating the Sadean source material by direct analogy and prognostic exploitation. The infernal circle of madness, excrement, and blood thus became a criticism of "neo-capitalism" via pornographic means; the "neo-fascism" of this "neo-capitalism" was itself analyzed using proto-fascist means. In a review of the film (*Le Monde*, June 15, 1976), Roland Barthes accused this exploitation of betraying the potentiality of the text. See Manfred Hermes, "Indirekt frei," *Texte zur Kunst*, no. 55 (September 2004): 134–41. Foucault also expressed skepticism about this film. Interestingly, in an interview for *Cinématographe* ("Sade, Sergeant of Sex," December 1975), he contrasts the conception of the body in Werner Schroeter's *The Death of Maria Malibran* (1972) with that in *Salò*. In Michel Foucault, *Aesthetics, Method, and Epistemology*, ed. James D. Faubion, trans. Robert Hurley et al. (New York: New Press, 1998), 223–28.

Kinks in the Historical

> We tend to forget what a secret complicity there was between the mid-1920s and the color black.
> —Edmonde Charles-Roux, *Chanel: Her Life, Her World, the Woman behind the Legend*

> Giving the freedom and generating the desire to formulate pain.
> —Rainer W. Fassbinder

Historicity is a central issue in Fassbinder's films, including those with a contemporary focus. Consequently, historicity cannot be approached in *BA* through the film's quality as a "costume drama," nor via any specific cinematographic qualities, nor even in terms of narrative technique.

As a shortcut to a broader view, we might take a text on Brecht by Roland Barthes from the 1950s, replacing Brecht with Fassbinder and theater with cinema or film: Fassbinder's cinema is predominantly a cinema of the present, but this present is never timeless, it is a historical present comprising an axis of collective events of national or global significance. But here, too, these major historical events of our time are not subjected to *explanation*. Between the explanation and expression of human alienation, Fassbinder develops an intermediate level addressing the issue of lucidity. His work is neither historical cinema nor action cinema; it continually presupposes both history as a source of explanation and action as an antidote to alienation. This is also presumably why opinion on Fassbinder is so often divided: his cinema strikes the partisan as too aesthetic, the aesthete as too partisan. In reality, and especially in Fassbinder's work, history is a general category: it is everywhere, but in a diffuse, non-analytical way; it is spread out, it sticks to human misfortune, being coessential with it like the back of a sheet of paper with its front. What Fassbinder asks us to look at and judge, however, is the front, a sensitive surface that consists of suffering, injustice, alienation, and hopelessness. Rather than making history an object, even a tyrannical one, Fassbinder makes it a general requirement for thinking. For him, basing a film on history is about more than expressing the true structures of the past. It also means denying human characters any essence and human nature any reality that is not historical, and believing that there is no eternal evil, but only individual evils that can be remedied; in a word, handing over man's destiny to man himself. (End of modified quote.)[1]

Apart from the conclusion in the final sentence, all of what Barthes writes here fully applies. Over time, this approach allowed Fassbinder to isolate and study the "German condition" and its outward manifestations: hatred of foreigners and Jews (*Katzelmacher, In a Year of 13 Moons*), immigration (*Love Is Colder Than Death, Ali: Fear Eats the Soul*), left-wing opportunism (*Mother Küsters Goes to Heaven, The Third Generation*), Nazi megalomania (*Lili Marleen*), the dilemmas and corruptions of the postwar years (*The Marriage of Maria Braun, Lola*). And he anchored all this in subjective mindsets, mentalities, feelings, object relations, and modes of perception (of the various sections of the German bourgeoisie). In his films, "history from below" could only be a history where everyone is involved as both victim and perpetrator.

1 Roland Barthes, "Brecht, Marx et l'Histoire" (1957), in *Oeuvres complètes, tome I, 1942–1965* (Paris: Éditions du Seuil, 1993), 753–54.

2 In *BA* Fassbinder only makes a brief appearance, hidden under a hat and in thick shadow. In other films he often referenced himself far more openly. In *In a Year of 13*

In Fassbinder's films, history is not something that has passed and ceased to be present, something that might become the subject of an impersonal narrative. A further level of presentness not mentioned by Barthes (because it plays no part in Brecht's plays) is a more specific subjectivization, the introduction of "I." This might be confusing, as it seems to confirm the abovementioned silly stereotypes of Fassbinder reception in Germany that saw his films as nothing but a doggedly cultivated form of egoism.

On the other hand, speaking about *BA*, Fassbinder himself confirmed these stereotypes when he declared, "I am Biberkopf."

Films do not make it easy to maintain a degree of abstraction (even if it is just the distinction between narrator and author that is taken for granted with regard to literary texts). As soon as a director appears in his own film or includes any form of self-reference, it becomes well nigh impossible to tell person and role apart and not to read them as just more proof of the enduring presence of the authorial function.[2] But this gesture of identification with a character in a novel, borrowed from Flaubert ("Madame Bovary, c'est moi."), can also be seen as a way of saying "I" without meaning "oneself."[3] After all, this "I"

Moons, Ingrid Caven is lying on a bed zapping between television channels showing *We Won't Grow Old Together* (Maurice Pialat, 1972), a TV report about Pinochet ("In the years that followed, his supporters say, Chile was transformed, from chaos to order—to discipline"), and a TV interview with Fassbinder, in which he speaks about his childhood. In his *Germany in Autumn* episode, on the other hand, he allowed fictional aspects to break into a primarily autobiographical setup: filmed at his home, featuring his mother and his lover, he not only bares his private life, but also gets physically naked.

3 On this, Gérard Genette writing about Proust: "Proust himself did not fail to get angry at the too-facile conclusions people drew from his narrative choice: 'As I had the misfortune to begin my book with *I* and could not change it anymore, I am "subjective" in aeternum. If I had begun instead, "Roger Mauclair was occupying a summer house," I would be classified "objective."' (to J. Boulanger, 30 November 1921, *Correspondance générale* [Paris, 1932], III, 278)." Gérard Genette, *Narrative Discourse: An Essay in Method*

relates to a figure not invented by Fassbinder himself, a character who, as described above, displays a highly contradictory blend of character traits. In this light, the first person is shifted into the realm of the doppelgänger, as something only relevant inside the act of storytelling.

Besides his claim of "Biberkopf, c'est moi," however, Fassbinder never says "I" in *BA*.[4] Although his voice is heard throughout, this presence—one of many narrative voice-overs—remains bodiless, devoted entirely to the oral aspect of language, and to the literary text of another author (that was only altered, if at all, by some melancholy warming-up due to the specific quality of Fassbinder's voice). Fassbinder's particular "making speak" did not "subjectively" open up, shape, or monopolize the literary material, as this "subjectivization" was staged on the material's own terms by transferring it into the film largely unchanged.

The key mode of production and updating here is "repetition." Discontinuity is generated by preserving the continuity (of discontinuity) in the original. Inserting reading itself into this form of narrative as a fracture allowed Fassbinder to comment without commenting and to symbolize without having to present himself as the master of this symbolism.[5]

(Ithaca, NY: Cornell University Press, 1980), 249. Proust himself on the same topic, this time in literary form: "Now she began to speak; her first words were 'darling' or 'my darling', followed by my Christian name, which, if we give the narrator the same name as the author of this book, would produce 'darling Marcel' or 'my darling Marcel.'" Marcel Proust, *In Search of Lost Time*, vol. 5, *The Prisoner and The Fugitive*, trans. Carol Clark (London: Penguin, 2003), 64.

4 Such a reference is there in the convoluted title of the final episode and its breakdown into ten lines: "Fassbinder / Berlin Alexanderplatz / 14 / My Dream / of / the Dream of / Franz Biberkopf / by / Alfred Döblin / An Epilog."

5 One of the great idiocies of Fassbinder reception is the way it has asserted and perpetuated an image of the greatest narcissist and self-promoter in cinema history for someone whose interventions gave him an almost unequaled right to say "I." On this

Although Fassbinder appropriated Döblin's material to a large extent, the historicizing movement does not run a predetermined course. The past is not suited, in and of itself, to being endlessly recycled. And even if Fassbinder did take his cue from the subliminal lines or missed opportunities of the 1920s as they appear in the novel, his film adaptation is nonetheless as far removed from the reawakening of something that can be nostalgically enjoyed as it is from an arbitrary analogy between the political realities of the time and those of the present day (Baader-Meinhof, erosion of the Left).[6]

Fassbinder's historicizing creates divides of a different kind. Rather than referring solely to the 1920s, the period between the book's publication (1929) and the making of the series (1979)

point, as elsewhere, there are similarities with the work of Martin Kippenberger, who also used first-person narratives as the basis for historicizations. The fate of this method is that it makes it hard to identify anything beyond "self-portrayal" and "self-promotion." Those who tread this path must reckon with being belittled and having anecdotes about them live on indefinitely. Even an early death does not necessarily alter this. In Kippenberger's case, things have changed in recent years, only to be replaced by the more glamorous but no less dubious yardstick of record prices paid for his artworks. See Manfred Hermes, *Martin Kippenberger* (Cologne: DuMont, 2005).

6 In spite of certain similarities and comparable breaks, the two postwar periods were ultimately too different. The aggressive state of domestic politics in the Weimar Republic with its various civil war–type events is hardly comparable with the period of consolidation and suppression of the recent past after 1945. In West Germany, the extreme Right tended to be integrated into the political system, while considerable portions of the left-wing and communist spectrum were transferred to East Germany or marginalized with bans—hence the extent of amnesia with regard to the Nazi past and the Holocaust, and the refusal to pursue any of the emancipatory projects of the 1920s. More striking is the fact that many of the social aspects addressed in *BA* are more topical today than they could possibly have been in 1979. At that time, West Germany had only around one million unemployed, welfare cuts were only just being prepared, and nationalist discourse was not widespread. Whereas now we are seeing a more unjust distribution of wealth, the soup kitchens of the 1920s have returned under new names, and German politics, both at home and abroad, has become more aggressive, slyly returning to the use of military means.

is also taken into account, given a specific charge, and drawn into the virtual focus of the film.[7] The resulting shift imposes a new time frame on Döblin's material, overriding its internal time structures.

This does not mean that the societal conflicts, structural injustices, and historical horrors lose their validity. Nowhere is it denied that history is a continuum of repression and unhappiness, that both material and spiritual living conditions are unbearable—in fact this is one of the basic assumptions in *BA*. (In *BA*/7 the narrator reads a letter from a mentally ill woman: "I'm tormented by the thought of doing something wrong and causing harm as a result.")

There are many references to the concrete political situation in Germany in the 1920s—the militarism, the aggressive nationalism, the persecution and continual criminalization of the Left. A small pointer is given in the background of a street scene in *BA*/5: on the top of a double-decker bus a group is broken up by police and red pamphlets flutter through the air. At a prominent moment toward the end of *BA*/4, Fassbinder accepts a break in the diegetic unity of the film, showing a poster that calls for protest against a famous political trial that took place in 1931: "Disgrace! Guardian of freedom and guarantor of peace Carl von Ossietzky sentenced. Come to the rally on December 22, Alexanderplatz."

Elsewhere, a more varied light is cast on prevailing political conditions. Toward the end of *BA*/9, Willy takes Biberkopf to an anarcho-syndicalist meeting. The speaker denounces parlia-

7 The fact that *BA* is not about faithfully reconstructing a bygone age is confirmed by a discrete but telling anachronism: in one of the film's few modernist interiors—"Pums' luxurious office"—the furniture includes steel and leather office chairs on rollers. Too inconspicuous to disturb the diegetic coherence of the scene, they do so nonetheless, as these props are examples of office design from the 1970s.

mentary democracy and the restriction of the right to strike, calling for an election boycott. ("The Socialists don't seize political power; political power has seized the Socialists. … Because the voters are tied down by legalities, and legalities mean coercion, the brute force of the ruling classes. No one is meant to notice. … The bourgeoisie and the Socialists and the Communists are happy and shout in chorus: all blessings come from above. … The parliamentary system prolongs the misery of the working classes.")

After the meeting, the two friends start talking to a worker who was also present. He cites the slaves who built Egypt's royal graves. ("European workers labor for decades with machines to heap up some private fortune. Progress? Maybe. But for whom?") Such hackneyed phrases give the sharp-tongued Willy the cue he has been waiting for: "Tell me, please, what is the difference between you and some Social Democrat?" The worker is put on the defensive, but this much he knows: one is either exploiter or exploited, one does honest or dishonest work, one is either for or against the proletariat. Now it is Biberkopf who notices the contradiction: "Your honest work is slavery. … And that's what you call direct action? It's just talk. Talk and more talk, yet you go to work and make the capitalists stronger. … You make shells for them, which they later use to shoot you dead. … I shouldn't do any work, according to your theory. I'm not boosting any capitalists. … You've got to stand on your own two feet. … I'm self-sufficient." The worker: "I was talking about refusing to work; but to do that, you've got to have a job first." Biberkopf, energetically: "And that's what I refuse to do." Worker: "We have to set up militant organizations." Biberkopf counters again: "On the one hand, you preach and say you're against every system, against any kind of order and all organizations. And then you want to set up militant organizations!" Worker: "You don't know what's important for the proletariat: solidarity."

How does the narrative relate to these forms of political "consciousness raising"? They are certainly taken into consideration; they are recognized as legitimate, necessary, and above all as existing social forces. The series of photographs in the opening sequence also show which social viewpoint Fassbinder has chosen and where his sympathies lie. But however sensible they may be, the utopian demands set out here are never granted any final validity. Döblin's skepticism is reflected in certain renderings in Fassbinder's film that take on the status of interpretations. In his script, the anarchist event is relocated to a "condemned building," the most doctrinaire agitators are played by older, melancholy men, and compared with his playful, arrogant interlocutors, even the combative worker in this scene comes across as a rather miserable advocate of his own interests. In *BA*, then, such political arenas are presented as lost causes.

This in turn calls other certainties into question, such as the notion of a "counter-history" of the disenfranchised that opposes the continuum of exploitation. In *BA*, there is no room for this kind of identity politics. The film does not speak for a proletariat, nor does it offer compensation for historical injustices, however symbolic. Identification along the lines of "class" plays no part in the work of Döblin and Fassbinder, and there is also none between the fictional characters. The flat social stratification of the novel rules out the type of antagonistic constellations that could be used to deduce or illustrate social struggle. In *BA*, the dialectic of master and servant, that fixes the value and "dignity" of work in historico-philosophical terms, is reframed in a significant way: "masters" appear at best in the role of criminal or "john," each existing to be fleeced by the other. Almost everyone here is an exploiter, regardless of the social position from which they operate. The traction of class struggle as a model for conflict is correspondingly low here, if only because in times of high unemployment strikes fail as a means of exerting power, and because the relative contribution of labor to value creation becomes obvious.

But let us return to the scene from *BA*/9: After the anarchist meeting, Biberkopf and Willy drop in on Eva and Herbert. Biberkopf recites his new insights, first as if by rote and then more freely: "The idea's quite simple, really: the state, and that means the police, does more to help and protect the rights of people who already possess a lot anyway. And the others, those who do the work, don't even think of, I don't know, taking action against it all, or demanding their rights, or whatever."

In any case, Biberkopf has now had his first fix of politics. His friends—she a well-heeled prostitute, he a minor-league criminal—counter Biberkopf's inflammatory talk with bourgeois values. (Eva: "Don't make me laugh! What would become of the world without order?") Having contradicted the gray-haired worker as an act of defiance, for the pleasure of provoking, or for perfectly good reasons, as he speaks to Eva he is now equally resolute in advocating the other man's position—something he himself is surprised by: "Isn't it strange that it's possible to talk and think for and against the same thing at the same time? I think it's strange."

Positions, beliefs, and opinions are mutable and context-specific; they, too, are poses and representations of social norms.[8] Biberkopf's indecisiveness points to ambivalences that are also present in *BA* as a whole. The scenes in the "condemned building" and at Eva's apartment are disturbed by numerous interventions and accretions in which other economies impose their demands.

8 In an interview with Jacques Grant (1974), when asked whether he understood his work as political, Fassbinder said, "Yes, but not in the same way as Brecht or a political party. Because I really don't know what is true at this precise moment. I think there is no real point of reference for my films; I can't say that there is an ideology somewhere in the world that matches my position or my indecisiveness." Fischer, *Fassbinder über Fassbinder*, 324.

At the start of the anarchist meeting comes the intertitle "The German Reich is a republic, and anyone who doesn't believe it will get shot in the neck." Then, while the docile audience is regaled with well-known Bakuninisms, Biberkopf's attention is distracted by the spontaneous memory of Mieze licking his hand and sucking his thumb. In the course of the polemic, the group drifts into an adjacent room within the ruined factory. There is a seesaw and a swing, like in a children's playground. The old worker still wants to know the same thing: "Out with it! What kind of job do you have?" Meanwhile, Franz and Willy pounce on the toys, swinging and seesawing as they continue their discussion. Fassbinder intervenes in voice-over: "There is a reaper whose name is Death. Both the birds of the heavens and the beasts: all gone." The worker insists: "And what are you doing here anyway if you're a capitalist?" Biberkopf: "I want to reduce Jerusalem to rubble and the abode of jackals, and lay waste the cities of Judah, so that no one can dwell in them." The worker: "That's just an excuse."

While it may be an excuse on the level of communication, on the narrative level it breaks the unity of the scene with a strong, overriding objection. It is no longer only emotions or libidinal compensations (pleasure, fun, mockery) that stand in the way of utopianism and its tiring attempts at indoctrination. Even solid arguments against endlessly deferring demands or for thinking about new forms of economy and community lose their force.

This Old Testament insertion, of which *BA* contains many others, introduces a transcendence whose timeless force pushes aside such profane things as solidarity, discontent, or personal experience of injustice and exploitation, even happiness and sexual pleasure. The anarchist idea of a general strike competes here with a different sphere, but one that can be attributed to a similar mindset. And in the 1920s both were referred to as "myth."

Thus, although it was customary at this time to underpin one's searching for truth with would-be archaic abstractions, here we see the concrete form this took. The Old Testament also dictated Döblin's own violence threshold and shaped his notion of a radically different order that "leaps out of history and attains a stable perfection."[9]

God's Particular Affinities

It is no coincidence that Walter Benjamin wrote of Franz Biberkopf that he is "consumed by a hunger for destiny." As well as revealing parallels between Döblin's and Benjamin's thinking, this assessment also permits a weighty reference to Benjamin's essay "Critique of Violence." In this notorious text, he attempted to frame the political, with its issues of violence, revolution, and the law, in theological terms. Revolution is like divine violence; it happens, manifesting as a catastrophic blow, beyond calculability: "Less possible and also less urgent for humankind, however, is to decide when unalloyed violence has been realized in particular cases."[10] It can never be identified "as such," but only by its "incomparable" effects. Incomparable here means "unmediated" and removed from representation. This excludes worldly authorities (parliamentary democracy, positive law, language in its naming function), but not the big criminal, the dictator, or the general strike as a tool in the political struggle. "If the existence of violence outside the law, as pure immediate violence, is assured, this furnishes the proof that revolutionary

9 This is how Carl Schmitt quotes Döblin from memory, in *Glossarium: Aufzeichnungen der Jahre 1947–1951* (Berlin: Duncker & Humblot, 1991), 83.

10 Walter Benjamin, "Critique of Violence" (1924), trans. Edmund Jephcott, in *Reflections: Essays, Aphorisms, Autobiographical Writings*, ed. Peter Demetz (New York: Schocken, 1986), 300.

violence [...] is possible, and by what means."[11] In 1940, having long since been influenced by Marxism, Benjamin reduced this impact of divine-revolutionary violence that establishes justice without law, to the following pithy historico-philosophical maxim: "The tradition of the oppressed teaches us that the 'state of emergency' in which we live is not the exception but the rule. We must attain to a conception of history that it is in keeping with this insight. Then we shall clearly realize that it is our task to bring about a real state of emergency."[12]

In the grand subproletarian hallucination that is *BA*, and in the divine judgment it hands down to Biberkopf, Döblin too clearly created a stage for this "exceptional," "real state of emergency," using similar figures of thought. For the violence that may descend, inexplicably, on anyone at any time, thus founding a new order, is also present here. After several years inside, Biberkopf leaves prison. He has done his time for manslaughter, and now he intends to live by the law. But after the punishment imposed by the state, a new cycle awaits him, as Fassbinder clearly states in the title of the very first episode: "The punishment begins."

It is not as if these affinities have gone unnoticed and their implications uncriticized. Thomas Mann devoted his novel *Doctor Faustus* (1947) to them, portraying the attitudes of a specific milieu that was influential in Germany in the years on either side of World War I. In their flirtation with the archetypal and

11 Ibid.

12 Walter Benjamin, "Theses on the Philosophy of History" (1940), in *Illuminations: Essays and Reflections*, ed. Hannah Arendt, trans. Harry Zohn (New York: Schocken, 1969), thesis 18, p. 257.

13 At the end of chapter 34, Mann added a seemingly remote yet potent example of the German tendency toward the atavistic and toward "radical elimination" from the field of dentistry: during the nineteenth century, the technique for root treatments was highly developed, but the early twentieth century saw a return to pulling out diseased teeth.

the primal, their aestheticized cult of barbarism, "profanity," and "objectivity" (why language? embrace things!), he saw not only a descent of Nietzscheanism into banality, but also an intellectual anticipation of the Nazi regime.[13]

Adorno, who was also interested in "the directions of the dark drives of the intelligentsia before 1933,"[14] judged Expressionism in similar terms. Yet Döblin himself is mentioned just once in his writings, rather unfavorably: "Today tragedy has been dissipated in the void of the false identity of society and subject, the horror of which is still just fleetingly visible in the vacuous semblance of the tragic. But the miracle of integration, the permanent benevolence of those in command, who admit the unresisting subject while he chokes down his unruliness—all this signifies fascism. Fascism lurks in the humaneness with which Döblin allows his protagonist Biberkopf to find refuge, no less than in films with a social slant."[15]

In 1980, based on the same assumptions, W. G. Sebald added a far more thorough critique of Döblin that amounted to a complete demolition. For Sebald, Döblin's oeuvre appeared as a collection of technical and artistic shortcomings, his character flawed and stricken with ideological dilemmas.[16] Out of pure "cultural radicalism," he writes, Döblin opposed the "centralism of the reigning political forces and their fetishization of organizations, seeking salvation in an anti-bureaucratic, anti-

14 Theodor W. Adorno, *The Jargon of Authenticity*, trans. Knut Tarnowski and Frederic Will (Evanston, IL: Northwestern University Press, 1973), 5.

15 Theodor W. Adorno and Max Horkheimer, *Dialectic of Enlightenment*, ed. Gunzelin Schmid Noerr, trans. Edmund Jephcott (Stanford, CA: Stanford University Press, 2002), 124.

16 Winfried Georg Sebald, *Der Mythus der Zerstörung im Werk Döblins* [The myth of destruction in the work of Döblin] (Stuttgart: Ernst Klett, 1980), 5. Further page references are cited in the text.

parliamentary doctrine that put its faith in the spontaneous revolutionary quality of the masses" (27). For the "restless," "disturbed" petit bourgeois wandering indifferently in the political, the scenes of "apocalyptic violence and destruction" and the "addiction to extremely cruel scenes" (134) were merely artistic compensation for fears of impoverishment and loss of social status (34). What presents itself as an "act of literary terrorism" is in fact "regressive longing" that "overran the attempts at enlightenment" (154). Although Sebald occasionally tempers his equation of "Döblin's avant-gardism rebelling against conventional concepts of literature" with the "praxis of fascist propagandists" (129), he then continues as follows: "What Döblin's work rhetorically evokes in the way of apocalypses and other images of the destruction of life obeys the same teleology as the desire of the fascists. [...] The author's guilt lies in his acceptance and dissemination of the monumental utopia of death contained in this apocalyptic rhetoric, a guilt he shares with politicians and ideologues," as a result of which "the aims of literature and politics are revealed as identical" (160).

There is no doubt that Döblin was implicated in these "dark drives." [TALES OF A LONG NIGHT] It may be helpful at this point to compare Sebald's critique with a text written a decade later. In his engagement with Benjamin's "Critique of Violence," Derrida chafed against similar questions but arrived at a more involved and less prickly statement of displeasure. Derrida, too, repeatedly mentions his difficulties with this "strange text," but they are more in the vein of inhibitions; he calls Benjamin's essay uneasy, enigmatic, dark, "terribly equivocal," but also "fascinating."[17]

What was so fascinating here? For one thing, the many analogies that existed in 1920s Germany between extreme left-wing and proto-fascist thinking (the examples he cites include Martin Heidegger, Carl Schmitt, and Franz Rosenzweig) on themes such as "destruction," rejection of parliamentarianism and the Enlightenment, and above all, in Benjamin's case, the notion of justice without law. And, finally, the fact that so many of the intellectuals involved with this thinking were, as Derrida said of Benjamin, "in a certain fashion, Jewish."

What Derrida found most disturbing about this "Judeo-German psyche" (977), however, was this: "The possible complicity between all these discourses and the worst (here the final solution)" (1045). The idea, then, that in Benjamin's remarks (on "true" revolution, lawmaking and law preserving, "pure means" and "just causes," violence and power, the mythical and the divine, representation and immediacy), the consequence and end point of this "sovereign" violence and the notion of a redeemed history might just as well be Hitler, the Nazi state, and Auschwitz—and the idea that Benjamin might actually have prefigured this. Derrida's uneasy conclusion: "What I find [...] the most redoubtable, indeed (perhaps, almost) intolerable in this text, even beyond the affinities it maintains with the worst [...] is a temptation that it would leave open. [...] The temptation to think the holocaust as an uninterpretable manifestation of divine violence insofar as this divine violence would be at the same time nihilating, expiatory and bloodless, says Benjamin, a divine violence that would destroy current law through a bloodless process that strikes. [...] It is at this point that this text, despite all its polysemic mobility and all its resources for reversal, seems to me finally to resemble too closely [...] the very thing against which one must act and think, do and speak" (1045).[18]

17 Jacques Derrida, "Force of Law: The 'Mystical Foundation of Authority,'" trans. Mary Quaintance, *Cardozo Law Review* 11 (1990): 919–1045. Individual page references are cited in the text.

18 In Mann's *Doctor Faustus*, Chaim Breisacher is the central figure in this proto-fascist "new objectivist" milieu, and Mann referred to him elsewhere as a "Jewish fascist": "The

Real Violence, the Violent Real

As all this shows, Fassbinder sewed long shadows to his heels with his choice of material. Moreover, as well as taking on Döblin's dark ideas and motifs unaltered, he also confirmed them in other works, most drastically in *In a Year of 13 Moons.*

Whereas in *BA*, the slaughterhouse motif is rendered only in a sequence of black-and-white photographs from the 1920s, in *13 Moons* Fassbinder filmed at a real location. While Elvira tells her life story in voice-over, Volker Spengler and Ingrid Caven stroll past cows waiting to die, then past corpses rolling out of a steel box to be gradually broken down into "meat." Before this scene, Caven (as Rote Zora) objects: "But striking animals, of all things, my dear, it's against life." To which Elvira replies, in a sweet and almost childish voice but with heightened theatricality: "Oh no it's not against life, it's life itself, the blood that steams, and death that gives the animal's life meaning, and the smell as they die, and they know full well that it's coming, death. … When I was young, I had the same revulsion as you. Today I understand the world better. Come with me, I'll show you, you have to smell, see the beauty and hear the screams. The screams for mercy."

Bearing this in mind, the darkened picture in *BA*, which at first glance seems so incongruous with Döblin's "modernity,"

frightfully clever playing of atavistic cards, a radical conservatism […] where the avant-garde coincides with the reactionary. […] It was through this very Breisacher that I first came into touch with the new world of anti-humanity." Thomas Mann, *Doctor Faustus* (1947), trans. H. T. Lowe-Porter (Harmondsworth: Penguin, 1968), 274.

19 This issue of light has been rationalized in very different ways. Harry Baer: "In the 1920s, there was far less electrical light than we have today; we were thinking of the films of Josef von Sternberg" (interview, May 28, 2009); a black-and-white film in color (as Fassbinder was known to put it). An explanation more in keeping with the usual reception in Germany went as follows: "The darkness that dominates the film is the sign of an egocentric reading of the novel." Christian Schärf, *Alfred Döblins "Berlin Alexanderplatz"*

may hint at deeper links; for example, to a dark surrealism of transgression and excess à la Georges Bataille. Fassbinder could thus be said to have reduced the photonic energy of his film to the conditions of this darkness.[19]

The functional core here, however, consists of trauma and pain. For Döblin, trauma was a wedge that is driven into the body by the violence of reality, making it a wonderfully, distinctly, and uniquely precise means of cognition. Unlike memory, which is capable of fabricating the past and inserting any number of gaps, pain, because it presupposes a specific object, gives access to areas that otherwise remain separate or unresolved.[20] What happens there is so violent and overwhelming that no protective shield (on the side of the subject) can withstand it.

Using the elements provided by Döblin, Fassbinder also constructed a historical arc of his own. While in Döblin's work, the action unfolds abstractly and timelessly between concepts like guilt, punishment, damnation, and redemption (in an arena marked out by Ida's murder, narcissism, and militarism), in Fassbinder's film it is shifted, by the act of repetition and the bracketing of the period between 1929 and 1979, into another

(Mainz: Franz Steiner, 2001), 35. The "remastering" of *BA* in 2007 should also be mentioned here. As well as removing fluff from the original 16 mm positives and correcting some image wobble, the dubious, probably scandalous decision was made to significantly brighten up the whole film. With this move, Fassbinder's estate, usually so keen to mute and blunt the image of its charge, conformed, three decades after the original broadcast of the series, to the aesthetic criteria of the tabloid press that at the time cried in unison: "But we can't see anything!"

20 The masochistic element in Döblin's novels has often been the subject of disconcerted remarks: "Humanity is permitted here only in the form of suffering, of transgression, of extreme baseness. What Döblin presents here is a grotesque *humilitas.* [...] Pleasure is taken in extreme social decline, in being tortured, generalized sadism is outdone by masochism, power turns to impotence, economy to mysticism." Dorothee Sölle, *Realisation: Studien zum Verhältnis von Theologie und Dichtung nach der Aufklärung* (Darmstadt: Luchterhand, 1973), 305–6.

dimension—that of National Socialism and the total violation, the most irrationally rational and absolutely inconceivable, the mass production of deaths and the dead, devised and executed on an industrial scale by Germans, now generally referred to as the Holocaust.

For Fassbinder, the task of fictionality here is to set the stage for a game with high stakes and to poke the spots where it hurts (or should hurt). This means that even if his call to risk more masochism is not addressed to the viewer as a "pervert," one has reason enough (as a German) to recognize the past as something to be suffered and to accept it as a task that has yet to be completed.[21]

Becoming Jewish, in a Certain Fashion

Fassbinder's contribution takes the form of a debenture, an obligation of debt, performed as a rotation around a "Jewish" axis. Here small compensations—like fashioning new representations of the "Jewish" dimension eradicated from Germany—do not suffice.[22] Instead, the "Jewish" dimension is to be under-

21 Largely ignored by German critics, the theme of "masochism" was only focused on by Anglo-American critics (Silverman, Rentschler, Crimp, Bersani, Burgoyne); its possible political function chiefly discussed by Silverman. But even these (mostly academic) American readings often failed to go beyond a figurative level (Silverman, *Male Subjectivity at the Margins*). Elsaesser, on the other hand, applied psychology to matters that possess only psychoanalytical significance (although the following quote refers to Fassbinder's early films): "In Fassbinder's melodramas, too, the heroes, because they are totally in agreement with the values that victimize them, are victims without knowing it. [...] By representing over and over again [...] a masochistic identification with an idealized oppressor or the tyranny of an idealized self-image, Fassbinder points to the masochistic side in cinematic identification generally." Thomas Elsaesser, *New German Cinema: A History* (London: Macmillan, 1989), 138–39.

22 Although this is also happening here: not only is this film based on the work of a writer who was Jewish, "in a certain fashion," there are also a number of "Jewish" characters, added to which Fassbinder preserved Döblin's "Hasidic" attribution of a healing function to storytelling. [Jewish matters: Appropriation of Tradition]

stood, integrated, or recast as something discarded by German history. Fassbinder was able to achieve this "reintegration of history" without any input of his own, on the basis of the same gesture of appropriation—all the more easily because, astonishingly and uncannily, the motifs he needed were there in the original material: human and animal sacrifice, abattoir scenes, Döblin's "blood thirst" and his fascination with death, murder, and the mortuary.[23]

This rotation can be more clearly understood in the light of works Fassbinder made around the same time as *BA*, allowing conclusions about the series and about the novel itself, which was an important point of reference for Fassbinder long before he filmed it.[24] The works in question are the play *Garbage, the City, and Death* (written in 1974, premiered posthumously in 1987) and *In a Year of 13 Moons*. Within slightly shifted frameworks, both works interlink the same two elements: "The Rich Jew" and sacrificial death.

In the figure of The Rich Jew, Fassbinder synthesized real events in the Frankfurt of the time with an inverted version of the notorious scapegoat theory. The German bourgeoisie grants the "Jew" a license to do the dirty work, making the post-war cities even more uninhabitable than they already are. His invulnerability is part of the scheme, as any criticism can be brushed aside with accusations of anti-Semitism.[25]

23 Here the passage from *BA*/4 quoted above is particularly remarkable: "The importance of fats in nutrition: fat acts as a covering for bone protuberances and protects the tissue beneath against pressure and impact. That's why emaciated people complain of pains in their feet when they walk."

24 He employed central Döblinian motifs as early as *Love Is Colder Than Death* (1969) even if in crude and cluttered form.

25 In an open letter from March 28, 1976, Fassbinder explained: "The phenomenon itself, though on a different level, is nothing more than a recapitulation of conditions in the

[Jewish Matters: Garbage, the City, and Death] Even explained in this way, the creation of such a figure may be considered unfortunate. More decisive, however, is the fact that Fassbinder also worked in similar ways with preexisting forms, clichés, and attitudes elsewhere in his oeuvre. [Jewish Matters: Representation]

Leaving aside the stereotype brought into play by the name of the role, these property speculators are neither one-sided figures, nor are they the main characters in *Garbage* or *13 Moons.* Their names are Roma B. and Erwin/Elvira, respectively.[26] Roma is an aging prostitute with a fin de siècle–esque respiratory ailment. Her father, once a high-ranking Nazi, now works in a bar as a drag artist. The Rich Jew takes a liking to Roma, leading to an intimacy that might be called love if their detachment and jadedness permitted unreserved emotions. Roma becomes a wealthy woman, but she is tired of her life; her boyfriend/pimp has long since left her for a man. At the end, she asks The Rich Jew to kill her, a request she has already made to other johns. This disturbing conclusion has an equivalent in *13 Moons.*[27] The two works differ in their details,

eighteenth century, when only the Jews were allowed to lend money at interest, and this money-lending, which was often the Jews' only hope of survival, in the end merely gave ammunition to those who had more or less forced them to take up this activity and who were their real enemies." Fassbinder, "My Position on *Garbage, the City, and Death,*" in Töteberg and Lensing, *Anarchy of the Imagination*, 119.

26 And not all property speculators in his work are "Jewish." See *Lola*.

27 The plot unfolds along a synthetic but nonetheless sad German postwar biography, as a personal "history film" that is told as a voice-over: Erwin is the result of a fling during World War II. When his mother's husband returns from a POW camp, she puts Erwin into a home, where he soon learns to curry favor. Since his true gifts are not fostered, he is obliged to undertake an apprenticeship in an abattoir. He gets married, a child is born, and then, in spite of his heterosexuality, he falls in love with Anton Saitz, with whom he is also involved in "meat" trafficking (Saitz is also a vegetarian). Prompted by the other man's casual remark that he could love him if he were a woman, Erwin undergoes a sex change.

but in both cases enormous sacrifices are made. Roma sacrifices her life; Erwin sacrifices his penis and, finding this was meaningless, also chooses death (as Elvira).[28]

These cases of suicide and death-on-demand perform the abovementioned German-"Jewish" rotation in sacrificial ceremonies. In both cases, the model was supplied by Döblin's *BA*: there, too, the longing for death, the questioning of gender identity, and the acceptance of total physical damage are the phenomena that mark Biberkopf's fateful path and express his desire for Reinhold.

Although "Jews" are certainly always involved in these ceremonies, it is equally certain that Fassbinder's films were not intended to speak for "Jews." He was interested not in confirming "identities," but in symbolizations, an approach that produces meaning in relations and differences—but at a time when even representations of "Jewishness" didn't exist in Germany.[29] [JEWISH MATTERS: REPRESENTATION]

On this basis, Fassbinder made further unbearable demands on his audience. The dream sequence in *BA*/14 includes a reappearance of the Jewish sausage vendor who Biberkopf met while selling Nazi newspapers in *BA*/2. Now he is wearing a death-camp uniform with a swastika armband over his jacket. To a flabbergasted Biberkopf, he explains: "Oh, you mean

28 Watered-down versions of this constellation are also to be found in films addressed to a mass audience. In *Veronika Voss*, (the potentially Jewish) Dr. Katz supports the former Nazi film star's opium habit in order to get her hands on her inheritance. (Perhaps this version is not so watered down after all: shortly before her death, Dr. Katz says to Voss: "You. You don't want to die yet, do you? You may only die when I allow it." The others present all laugh uproariously.) In *The Marriage of Maria Braun*, the titular character dies at the peak of her own private economic miracle from the effects of "gas."

29 Some say that it was only with the screening of the American series *Holocaust* in West Germany, in 1979, that the historical fact in question became irrevocably anchored in the German consciousness.

the swastika? Yes, I wear it now, and with pride, Mr. Biberkopf. You wore it, too, back then." "Yes, I wore it, too, back then. But didn't you tell me you're Jewish?" "Sure. But that doesn't mean you have to take the wrong path. Now I'm on the right one!"[30]

Honoring Historical Obligations, Indirectly

All of this represents neither a simple reading of Döblin nor an easily acceptable "political" solution. In fact, Fassbinder offers no prospect of solutions whatsoever, since a settlement is not possible (I am still referring to the Holocaust here). For this reason there can be no love between the characters in *Garbage*, just as compensation or redemption are impossible on a historical level. If this were not the case, the word aporia would lose all meaning. Just because something cannot be resolved or represented, does not mean that it cannot be portrayed or that it should be ignored. Unlike the products of the mind, artistic productions must perform their acting out of unpleasant or painful content in full consciousness.

The result may be oppressive, repellent, or hard to carry out, but it does not lack transparency, rigor, or "enlightening" potential. It "honors obligations in a historical sense," but not in the way Adorno was calling for. No rules can be established for the impact made within artistic productions by real-world content or history. No nontraditional handing down of art-specific and formal problems, passed on from one generation to the next, could have settled these debts that Fassbinder had always been concerned with keeping open.

30 It's a dream sequence, for sure—Fassbinder's dream of the "Dream of Franz Biberkopf by Alfred Döblin"—but this passage is not to be found in Döblin's book.

31 How often, incidentally, did those on the Left declare him unfit to be called "left wing" (at a time when this reproach was the ultimate insult). One might also recall Straub/Huillet, who at some point added Fassbinder to their pompous list of porno-

Why something that had nothing at all to do with stereotypes and so much to do with a "sharp eye" for the monstrosities of German history was debated purely in terms of this accusation of anti-Semitism, always couched in the same terms, must therefore remain a mystery.

The fact that Fassbinder's films were at odds with then prevalent notions of enlightening, emancipative art production is easier to understand. He used none of the modest or hackneyed aesthetic commonplaces that at the time would have quickly marked him out as a "historical materialist," even though his work in fact represented a much subtler, more sophisticated and advanced version.[31]

His films did not make it easy for "politically" minded viewers because, in spite of a very clear position on the issues of the day, they could expect neither automatic solidarity with the disadvantaged and disenfranchised, nor offers of simple self-empowerment and hopeful projections of an ideal society or a redeemed history.[32]

This does not mean that impact, involvement, action, or change had become totally inconceivable. But Fassbinder gave a different form and direction to the political. His approach depends on "subjectivization," on submitting to something that can only be ineluctably realized in the greatest possible losses. *This* notion of involvement can hardly be managed in cultural terms, and could not be integrated into power structures of

graphic filmmakers, due to a suspicion of glamorizing fascism in *Lili Marleen* and his affiliation with West German producer Luggi Waldleitner.

32 Fassbinder on this topic: "When members of the proletariat come in contact with members of the bourgeoisie, then they are very quickly spoiled and they try to imitate them and lead a similar life. All classes betray their own character and favor the next higher. That's why we can wait a very long time for a real revolution in this world." In John Hughes and Brooks Riley, "A New Realism: Fassbinder Interviewed," *Film Comment* 11, no. 6 (November–December 1975): 14–17.

whatever kind. Fassbinder could never have arrived at a formula like "It is us," the "it" in question being "the Party," which in Brecht's *The Decision* is the guarantor of proletarization. The notion that any authority might claim the place of a godlike reason—of the kind that demands human sacrifices from on high in Brecht's gruesome agitprop play and even forces the victim to accept this necessity—is not acceptable within *BA*.

Although Fassbinder's staging of history is peopled by figures of a not essentially dissimilar subjectivization, he took into account a psychic and emotional dynamic that underlies relations of exchange and social ties. The result is an anticipatory moment that could be realized neither by the individual alone nor without the individual. Which is also why the last sentence of the modified Barthes passage quoted at the beginning of this chapter does not apply to Fassbinder's historiography. As we will see in the next chapter, believing "that there is no eternal evil but only individual evils that can be remedied; in a word, handing over man's destiny to man himself," is only an option here if it involves a more heteronomous approach to "action as an antidote to alienation."

Can You Dance an Aporia?

In a Year of 13 Moons includes a weird scene featuring a frantic mix of registers and a striking change of mood. It is set on the upper floors of an office block, with a good view of the Frankfurt skyline. This is the office where the "Jewish speculator" Anton Saitz helped to plan that very skyline. Now, however, he is killing time in tennis clothes with his advisers, bodyguards, and chauffeurs (because "bankruptcy is the best business at the moment"). Elvira, who, as Erwin, was once in love with Anton, apprehensively walks into the room, having gained entry with the code word "Bergen-Belsen." A screen is showing the "I Like to Hike" parade from *You're Never Too Young* (Norman Taurog,

1955). As well as being threatening, Saitz also has a playful side. He asks those present to act out the parade "once more." They imitate the mock military drill in the movie, and the beaten, sad, fearful Elvira cheerfully joins in. Then she stumbles, and Saitz leaps into the strong arms of his chauffeur and strikes a pinup pose. (Is this a "utopian" moment?)

On the Stage of Maximum Ambiguity

> But people are stones.
> —Marieluise Fleißer

> We know what we know.
> And we had to pay dearly for what we know.
> —Last intertitle in *BA*

Can you film aporias? How can one show what cannot be seen and what therefore escapes visual mediation? In Fassbinder's *BA*, this is shown in repetitions, exchanges, cyclical movements, and an insistence on damaging and self-damaging acts.

After his stay in prison, Biberkopf wants to become a new person but circumstances prevent his self-improvement. He is immediately drawn back into cycles that tie him more to the past than to the future. Before the story begins, he has dealt heavy blows to others, and now he must learn to be on the receiving end. He is betrayed, he is pushed in front of a car, he loses an arm, his life is under constant threat, and at the end his friend kills his lover. Biberkopf responds to all this with breakdowns, withdrawals, fainting, and hallucinations. After every setback, he gets back on his feet.

Cyclical movements also define Biberkopf's relationship with women and men. After his release, he visits a prostitute but is unable to perform. His impotence is overcome when he rapes the sister of his manslaughter victim Ida. His first lover is someone he meets by chance, while all the others are introduced to him by friends. After befriending Reinhold, he is pushed into a system of trading girlfriends: as soon as Reinhold tires of a woman, Biberkopf will take her off him. In this system, women are the currency between men, revealing the elementary structures of these particular elective kinships.[1]

Biberkopf's final cycle revolves around Mieze—a woman handpicked for him by his ex-lover Eva. Like Eva, Mieze works as a prostitute. Not only is Biberkopf obliged to share her with other men, she also turns him back into the pimp he has already been in an earlier life. Even the barkeeper of his regular bar notices that he is reliving old patterns: "You're back where you were again. Ida is now Mieze; you've lost an arm; and you've started drinking again, just as bad as before. And that means the same thing all over again, only worse. And then it'll all be over, Franz" (*BA*/9).

And confusingly, although Reinhold does everything he can to harm him, Biberkopf repeatedly says, "But it doesn't matter. I'm not mad at him because of it" (*BA*/13); "It's OK that the arm's gone. The arm had to go" (*BA*/7).

Detours toward Unpleasure

Why does Biberkopf accept his traumatizations? Why does he even welcome them? In her essay on *BA*, a puzzled Susan Sontag asked questions like these, repeatedly expressing her inability to understand Biberkopf's "odd docility": "After the amputation of his arm [Biberkopf] is strangely without desire for revenge."[2] But in fact, the thinking on which Sontag's disconcertment is based is discussed in *BA* itself. After his "accident," everyone in Biberkopf's entourage urges him to take revenge, or at least to claim compensation for the lost arm ("They must pay you a pension").

1 An explanation for this can be given in the words of Luce Irigaray, quoted by Kaja Silverman: "The use of and traffic in women subtend and uphold the reign of masculine hom(m)o-sexuality, even while they maintain that hom(m)o-sexuality in speculations, mirror games, identifications, and more or less rivalrous appropriations, which defer its real practice. Reigning everywhere, although prohibited in practice, hom(m)o-sexuality

Clearly, Biberkopf's docility follows a logic that is not calculating and economical. In this logic, the incomprehensible is actually the norm, as it revolves around something that really is hard to comprehend: desire and its structure.

However hard to grasp the structure of desire may be, cinematic productions do have the potential to access it in principle. And it has rarely been so persistently and lucidly dramatized as in the films of Alfred Hitchcock. Apart from anything else, his notions of the sexual were so profoundly developed that he was able to identify something thoroughly determined even in the simple physical attraction between two people. He knew that one always desires something else through the immediate object of one's love—and he accorded special importance to the connection between money, narcissism, and neuroses passed on from one generation to the next.

Even in his less polished films, Hitchcock was able to create monuments to the tortuous paths patrolled by desire, for example in *To Catch a Thief* (1955). John Robie, a one-time jewel thief, has retired to the Côte d'Azur. With her mother, Frances Stevens is on a grand tour of Europe, in search of a husband. A series of hotel robberies stirs things up and everyone assumes Robie is making a comeback. Stevens, who knows about Robie's past, wants to exploit this knowledge for her own little thriller. Thinking she knows what Robie wants, for their first intimate encounter she wears her most precious and

is played out through the bodies of women, matter, or sign, and heterosexuality has been up to now just an alibi for the smooth workings of man's relations with himself, of relations among men." In Silverman, *Male Subjectivity*, 239.

2 Susan Sontag, "Novel into Film: Fassbinder's *Berlin Alexanderplatz*" (1983), in *Where the Stress Falls: Essays* (New York: Farrar, Straus and Giroux, 2001), 127. Elsaesser, too, complained of problems with comprehension: "We never really understand why Reinhold did push Franz out of the speeding car"; "the viewer [is left] baffled at their motives or goals." Elsaesser, *Fassbinder's Germany*, 226, 219.

sparkling necklace. In this way, she ascribes to him the view she holds herself: people will only ever be attracted to her on account of her money. She expects Robie to steal what she herself considers to be her prize asset. What she doesn't know, however, and what Robie realizes, is that in this little game she is acting out her own self-contempt ("You're an insecure, over-pampered woman"). One key scene is magnificently devised. It is after dark and Stevens presents to Robie the frozen eruption of her diamond necklace (which both emphasizes and guards her décolleté) while outside, the sparks of a more generous and ephemeral firework display squirt off into the night sky. (The necklace she uses to incite Robie's greed is a replica; when the original is stolen, she is still not pleased.)

It is never only women, however, who are dragged from the morass of indifference and stupor in Hitchcock's films. Access to desire is blocked for all participants in the gender continuum, the price to be paid equally high. As sexual interest is only ever a point of departure, sudden events must be introduced to bring about an extraordinary disturbance of the peace and to trigger the superhuman efforts required to set the dramatic engine in motion. Robie would rather remain quietly retired; Stevens would rather go on being exempt from any serious form of exchange in her dealings with others.

This setup is often influenced by a third key element: dominant mothers. Onto the desires of their children they impress a special profile, grounding unrealistic demands and hindering access to love and a responsible position within society. Curtailing this maternal influence is a driving force in every second Hitchcock plot, with "marriage" as the culmination and true meaning of the adventure. Nonetheless, the formula of love or any other exchange between human individuals is updated: one must give what one doesn't have and take what the other cannot give.

This mother/son configuration also sheds some light on the conditions prevailing in *BA*. But the corners of the wife/husband/mother triangle are shifted. In *BA*, things are more abstract, demanding, and "German" than in Hitchcock—and where Döblin is concerned (though not Fassbinder), also less charming. In *BA*, there is no dominant mother, there are not even families, so there cannot be a "family novel." Biberkopf has little more from his father than his name.[3] But *BA* does deliver a take on a theme that became ubiquitous in the early twentieth century: the erosion of the paternal function and the position of the male.[4]

Fathers who are too weak, mothers who reinforce the existential anxiety of their children—one might think the outcome would be the same. But in contrast to Hitchcock (and this is in part what makes Döblin so uncharming) a particularly heavy signifier is brought into play: God.

This entity is represented in *BA* by Reinhold, as we are told in one episode title: "A Grim Reaper with Powers from Almighty God." Reinhold is an easily excitable, "explosive" character (after World War I, in his anarchist phase, he wanted to blow up a gasworks). As a criminal and law unto himself, he also has an advantage over Biberkopf in the form of a greater ruthlessness. As such, he performs the function of the father, bringing about traumatization. But Biberkopf always says: It doesn't matter, that's the way it had to be.

3 Fassbinder helped out here: "I tried to make Meck into a kind of father figure, although he may actually be younger than Franz. And Brigitte Mira plays his mother figure." Interview with Christian Braad Thomsen (1980), in Fischer, *Fassbinder über Fassbinder*, 484. And at one point (in *BA*/7) Biberkopf suddenly turns to Meck and asks, "Just one more question. I wanted to know if you ever had a father."

4 This overlaps with Döblin's own experience: in his childhood, his father left the family overnight.

In *BA*/11, a key phrase is introduced, emphasized by an intertitle and its repetition: "And while he's dancing with Eva, he dearly loves two people. One is his Mieze, whom he wishes could be there. The other is—Reinhold."

The relations outlined here would not be adequately described by the word "queer" even if it were not the blurry, all-purpose term it has now become. Biberkopf's desire encompasses variables somewhat grander than those on which notions of the "social constructedness of sexuality" are based.

The ties binding Biberkopf to Reinhold and those binding Reinhold to Biberkopf are not reciprocal or of the same order. Reinhold can cause greater damage; Biberkopf is positively asking to be injured.

An adjoining aspect here is the lack of reciprocity between the sexes. Women play a marginal role in the negotiation of truth—in *BA* it is conducted solely among men. And it is two men whose desire intersects and overshadows all of the film's other relationships. Maybe women aren't needed here because "there are men who are just as good as women."[5] The men in question are hysterics.

Hysteria

As my argument here regularly makes use of psychoanalytical terms and concepts, it should perhaps be made clear that this is not intended as a psychoanalytical reading or an autonomous theoretical work. I am merely tracing out what is already there in Döblin's *BA* and the extent to which Fassbinder used it. Without the amputation, there would be no need to speak of castration; without Biberkopf's symptoms, no mention of

5 Jacques Lacan, *The Seminar of Jacques Lacan*, ed. Jacques-Alain Miller, bk. 20, *On Feminine Sexuality, the Limits of Love and Knowledge, 1972–1973*, trans. Bruce Fink (New York: W. W. Norton, 1999), 76.

hysteria; without the affirmation of his own degradation, no need to speak of the mysterious dialectic of desire. And one must assume that Döblin introduced these motifs deliberately. After all, he was not only familiar with psychoanalytical theory, he was a specialist with clinical experience in the field, wrote several reviews of Freud's writings,[6] and underwent training analysis himself around 1920 (with Ernst Simmel). And by all accounts, he also used psychoanalytic methods in his own general medical practice.[7]

Fassbinder, in turn, was aware of Döblin's specialist background.[8] Noting and using the full range of issues present in the novel certainly called for a particular awareness on his part, and it would be interesting to know what this heightened sensitivity was based on. One can assume above-average skills in close reading, heightened powers of (self-)observation, and certain philosophical influences that may have acted as mediators (Spinoza, Schopenhauer, Nietzsche). But Fassbinder was also bold enough to make artistic use of his own anxieties. However, apart from isolated positive remarks on psychoanalysis ("Every

6 Alfred Döblin, *Kleine Schriften*, vol. 2 (Olten: Walter, 1990); Alfred Döblin, *Kleine Schriften*, vol. 3 (Zurich: Walter, 1999).

7 Döblin may have drawn on his clinical experience for a scene in a doctor's room, presenting a conflict between generations. Toward the end of the novel and in *BA*/14, Biberkopf is in a psychiatric ward. The doctors discuss the appropriate treatment. A young man wishes to try psychoanalytic methods. The senior physician takes Biberkopf for a fake; he also thinks there's nothing a bit of electroshock therapy can't cure: "It's better than all this blather. … The mind, the mind! Oh, this modern catchall for the emotions! Medicine on the wings of poetry!" The young doctor: "But that's just it, doctor. He's inhibited. In my opinion, it's the result of some blockage, but caused by mental factors: a loss of reality, disappointment, denial, then childish, impulsive claims on reality, unsuccessful attempts to restore his hold on it." "Nonsense! Mental factors, indeed!"

8 "Döblin's attitude toward his characters […] is, I would contend, in all likelihood influenced by Sigmund Freud's discoveries, even if Döblin disputed this on several occasions." Fassbinder, "Cities of Humanity," 166.

child should do one") and this film version of *BA*, there is little real evidence to support such assumptions.[9] Fassbinder not only noted the psychoanalytic influences in *BA*, he was also capable of expanding them on Döblin's terms.[10] This applies, for example, to the field of pregenital pleasures and drives during infancy. Although primary sources of pleasure do play an important part in Döblin's novel, enjoyment of motor functions and oral satisfaction can be portrayed to greater effect in film. In Fassbinder's *BA*, people are forever swinging, seesawing, spinning around in office chairs for the sake of the movement. While food and drink are devoured in huge quantities in the novel, too, it is only in the film that tongues are used not just to taste and speak, but also to entice and satisfy: women tongue glasses and suck on thumbs to invite usage of other orifices.[11] Biberkopf himself has more violent demands, expressed in his taste for biting his partner's neck. But all these incidences are

9 Fassbinder's portfolio of unfinished film projects also included *Moses and Monotheism*, Freud's speculative book on an Egyptian who gathers around him a people whose law and coherence is founded on the violent act of patricide (against Moses). Fassbinder's affirmation of psychoanalysis as a form of therapy is especially evident in *13 Moons*. Sister Gudrun: "Do you really think you need these memories, do you really think so?" Elvira: "Yes, Sister, I do." Before this, Seelenfrieda (Walter Bockmayer) tells Elvira and Rote Zora a story from her life: "Me, for example, I spent eight years in the nuthouse. … Set me straight, they did, made sure I stopped being so conspicuous and scaring little children. But the only thing that might really have helped … no way! 'Unfortunately, psychoanalysis is out of the question in your case, because you are an orphan.'" (The scene is overlaid with Suicide's screechy "Frankie Teardrop.")

10 On this point, too, American critics were more attentive. Ian Buruma: "Some of Fassbinder's visual inventions are brilliant elaborations on Döblin's own imagination." In "The Genius of Berlin," *New York Review of Books*, January 17, 2008.

11 In *BA*/12, there is a significant, very drastic detail, strongly distanced by the use of a long shot. Moments before the murder, Mieze and Reinhold are lying together on the forest floor like romantic lovers. As he looks down at her, a shining strand creates a link between their heads: almost invisibly, Reinhold dribbles saliva into Mieze's mouth. She accepts the fluid without resisting.

mere preliminaries to the more far-reaching pathologies that drive the plot: Döblin endowed Biberkopf with many attributes of the hysteric.

Freud's discovery of the psychic roots of hysteria laid the foundations for key concepts of psychoanalysis: the unconscious, the mechanism of fantasy and identification, conflicts of defense and repression, transference and desire. It was the case history of Dora that forced Freud to realize the complicated shifts of desire. The hysteric has trouble with abreaction. He can only love by proxy and on condition of remaining exempt from processes of exchange. He only dares to approach a homosexual object through identification with a person of the other sex.

Dora identifies with Mr. K. by adopting his desire for Mrs. K. But Mrs. K. "represents something that her father can love beyond her."[12] Dora wants what her father wants. She appropriates his object, but her homosexual desire (for Mrs. K.) masks a heterosexual one (for Mr. K.).

Concerning hysteria, Döblin was also able to work from experience, having published a study of his own on the subject: "Attention Deficits in Cases of Hysteria."[13] He describes the symptoms of Lina W., a "maid," as follows: "uncertainty of memory," partial amnesia, and "hallucinatory deliria"; Lina W. wanted "to get into the cupboard," dressed "back to front" (464), and saw "men without heads," including her father. Döblin interpreted these reactions as a fear of "sterility" (467). More-

12 "Mme K qui se présente comme quelque chose que son père [le père de Dora] peut aimer au-delà d'elle [de Dora]." Jacques Lacan, *Le seminaire IV: 1956–1957. La relation d'objet et les structures freudiennes* (Paris: Seuil, 1994), 110.

13 Alfred Döblin, "Aufmerksamkeitsstörungen bei Hysterie," *Archiv für Psychiatrie und Nervenkrankheiten* 45, no. 2 (March 1909): 464–88. Page-number references are given in the text.

over, he claimed, "restriction of the field of awareness" made Lina W. unable "to lift a large number of basic emotions over the threshold" (474). And, "as her attention is fragmented by focusing on one group of mental images, it takes on the heightened quality of a hallucination" (476).

Displacement of representations, reinforcement of ideas and mental images, not being able to lift something over the threshold, deliria, fear of sterility—all of this bears a strong resemblance to Biberkopf's symptoms. And then there are his unusual choices of partner.

Initial signs, still temporary in nature, are seen in the acute impotence of *BA*/1. Later, Biberkopf repeatedly loses his balance, feints, and, whenever his "masculinity" is under threat, he complains of unspecific pains. Just before he learns of Mieze's murder, he sits around in a stupor, wearing makeup and dressed in his girlfriend's clothes. Another time he says, "I can't move my legs anymore. It's just not possible. They just won't move anymore."[14]

Biberkopf's fits and seizures point to another kind of powerlessness. His desire directed toward Reinhold shows that lack of power is precisely what Biberkopf wants. He has Reinhold efface his "masculinity," but only on condition that Reinhold adopts the role of a superhuman authority that is therefore permitted to demand submission and that renders this submission acceptable. As such, Biberkopf is a lesser version of Daniel Schreber, even if Schreber strictly counts as a paranoiac. On one key point, however, Lacan's remarks on Freud's analysis of Schreber's *Memoirs of My Nervous Illness* also apply

14 Around 1980, Fassbinder repeatedly mentioned a planned novel. In a TV interview with Peter W. Jansen ("Lebensläufe," Südwestfunk, 1982) he outlined the contents: "It was to be the story of a man who suddenly finds himself unable to move, but after a course of self-analysis, he regains motor control."

to Biberkopf: adopting the female position in relation to his father goes against his narcissism, but castration "can no longer affect him once his partner has become God."[15]

When One's Partner Is God

When one's partner is God, then there is plenty of headroom. In order to include such absolute entities, Döblin had already used Old Testament motifs and the story of Job. There, too, a fate is inflicted and a subject seriously threatened.

In an early contact with the realm of downfall and death, Biberkopf is more inclined to see its grand and glorious sides. In *BA*/6, after his car accident, badly wounded and close to death, he launches into a jubilatory monologue on the contingency of human existence with a planetary slant: "When the sun rises and we are happy, one should actually be sad, for what are we really? The sun is 300,000 times bigger than the Earth. … We are a zero ourselves, absolutely nothing. It's ridiculous really, yet one's happy nevertheless. You come out onto the street, and feel strong. Colors emerge; people's faces come to life; and there are forms. … And it is a joy that we can look and see: that we can see these colors and the lines. … We take pleasure in a little warmth. We're happy that the flowers can grow." (And the narrator adds: "There is no cause for despair. When I continue with this tale, telling it to its bitter, frightful end, I shall often use these words: No cause for despair.")

By this point, Biberkopf has already been confronted with an outside that exists by itself and doesn't require observers. This outside can delight, but it can also crush, with a violence that cannot be assimilated and that breaches any protective barrier—something akin to trauma and castration. This sphere

15 Jacques Lacan, *The Seminar of Jacques Lacan*, ed. Jacques-Alain Miller, bk. 3, *The Psychoses, 1955–1956*, trans. Russell Grigg (London: Routledge, 1993), 89.

of sudden violence corresponds roughly to Heidegger's "primary being," to Lacan's "the real," Badiou's "event," and Benjamin's "shock." In *BA* it is represented in the figure of Reinhold, and it is precisely this aspect of sudden violence that Biberkopf's desire focuses itself upon.

Fassbinder often showed an interest in such overdeterminations. In *BA*, for example, radiance and splendor are always deployed in gruesome and macabre moments: the body in agony, in its raw physicality, or in a state of decomposition, is overlaid with sparkling highlights and glimmer. He would emphasize especially terrible, fateful, or horrifying moments by briefly freezing the scene, immobilizing the performers.

Other films, too, offered lessons in the acknowledgment of death and the sublime, most especially *In a Year of 13 Moons*. There, where the nineteenth century's historical obsession mixes with affect-driven punk, the lesson is touched on briefly with lines from Goethe's *Torquato Tasso* ("When something unparallel'd occurs / When something monstrous first arrests our sight, / The stagger'd spirit stands a moment still, / For we know nothing to compare it with") and at some length with Schopenhauer's *The World as Will and Representation* ("But it would be a great misunderstanding to see that as a negation of the will to live, to see suicide as an act of negation. Far from it: the negation of the will to exist is a bold affirmation of the will since negation means renouncing not life's sufferings but its joys. The suicide wants life and simply rejects the conditions under which he experiences it. The suicide does not renounce the will to live; he renounces life by destroying the manifestation of his own life").[16]

16 In an interview with Norbert Sparrow, Fassbinder said that the "body [learns], from the moment it leaves the womb, that it can die. When you accept that a part of life is death, you have no more fear of it, and you don't fear any other 'conclusions.'" *Cineaste* 8, no. 2 (Fall 1977): 20–21.

A Hell of a Fabrication

In the ninth and final chapter of Döblin's book, and the fourteenth and final episode of Fassbinder's film, the central conflicts are ultimately raised to an apocalyptic level. Here, Fassbinder ran the gamut of the constructive features of the dream. With all of the previously introduced characters, scenes, and narrative elements recombined as his dream material, he created a stage that openly acknowledges the reality of the film studio.

After numerous traumatizations, Biberkopf is struck another mighty blow. A new phase of wallowing, lamenting, and humiliations begins. At this high point, and at the end of the process of atonement and clarification, the "lessons" take the form of a therapeutic intervention. Biberkopf does his penance in the psychiatric clinic, where he lies around, motionless and delirious, refusing to eat or speak. He looks for his girlfriend's grave in a cemetery where he meets characters from the series in blurred and distorted versions, allowing them to engage him in dialogues of the dead.

At the same time, Biberkopf's life is evaluated behind his back by the guardian angels Sarug (Helmut Griem) and Terah (Margit Carstensen): "This man has unwittingly failed to grow up, Sarug. But he's about to now. And everyone who suffers from this rare misfortune has the tendency, when on the threshold of seeing and feeling, to gain this insight and then slip away and die." "One is never intrinsically strong, just by nature. You must have been through something. Strength has to be acquired. You don't know how you acquired it. Suddenly you're standing there, and things that are deadly to others are no longer a danger to you."

Then other good friends and old acquaintances appear and take turns rebuking Biberkopf, showering him with accusations, and pushing his delirium in a specific direction. Reinhold: "You were blind and cocky, and snobby to boot. … And the world should be as you want it. It's all quite different, my boy, quite different. Now you can see it. It couldn't care less about you, the world couldn't." And Meck: "No head, no eyes, no ears, no brain, with mad ideas, with cocky ideas."

In the forest first seen in *BA*/8 Biberkopf also meets Baumann again. In a pleated golden cloak he is now more easily recognizable as a caring Death, reprising the role he played more covertly in *BA*/4.[17] He blackens Biberkopf's face with soil and this time his litanies are delivered far more relentlessly: "How can a man thrive if he does not seek out death, true death, real death? Your whole life you've been safeguarding yourself. Safeguarding: that's man's fearful desire. And so everything stays as it is and doesn't move on. … And whatever you undertook, you clutched at the idea of strength; and that fixation still hasn't abated. But it's no use. You felt it yourself. It's no use. There comes the moment when nothing helps. Death does not sing you a gentle song." Then it is the turn of the rabbi Nachum: "When a guy has the word 'death' on his lips, no one can tear it from him. He'll turn it over in his mouth, and it'll be like a stone, a stony stone; and no nourishment will grow from it. In this way, many people have died. For them, there was no going on. They didn't know that they had to inflict but a single pain on themselves in order to go on, that only a small step was needed to go on. But they were unable to take that step."

Masculinity

These incisive changes that supposedly lead out of narcissism and into the arms of death are not so easy to bring about,

17 There the dialogue was as follows: "Did you lose your heart to nature? … In the roar of the youth movement? In the turmoil of politics?" Biberkopf: "I didn't lose it there." Baumann: "So you haven't lost it anywhere? Are you the type of person who doesn't lose his heart anywhere, but keeps it for himself, conserves it clinically, mummifies it?" Biberkopf: "Is death the end of everything?"

however. Letting go of illusions, claims, and ways of life is hindered by lethargy, and even the drives are conservative. It is far easier to eliminate annoying obstacles, and so Reinhold shoots Eva and her boyfriend Herbert, Lüders shoots the widow, while Biberkopf shoots Reinhold, who promptly turns into Ida.

It is no coincidence that Ida appears so frequently at this point. Although her killing took place before the plot gets underway, it underpins all of what takes place in the novel. Exploiting his masculine strength and physical power, Biberkopf played fate (as Reinhold later did with him). But this sudden *passage à l'acte* also reflected something that could not be assimilated. Ida wanted to break up with Biberkopf, mocking him and undermining his claim to omnipotence. (Due to its importance, this killing scene is repeated several times, in varying lengths, throughout the series.) He had "clutched at the idea of strength" rather too tightly, cooling libidinous energies, resisting ambivalences, and styling himself as a hard heart in a tough shell. Döblin's characterization might thus appear to match Klaus Theweleit's assumptions about militarily numbed fascist men in *Male Fantasies* all the better since Döblin, as already mentioned, was variously accused of indulging in similar tendencies.

On the other hand, for Döblin, no less than for Fassbinder, the standards of gender identity were an important starting point and target for attack.[18] Nothing could be remoter from the terrain of emotions shaped by fascism explored by Theweleit than the conditions depicted in *BA*. Although the figure of Biberkopf does correspond in part to the type studied by Theweleit, is it not so resolutely set in stone. After all, Döblin

18 Conversely, few directors have offered such an attractive range of "masculine" men. Fassbinder's films thus also contain the strongly erotic charge of an authoritarian, threatening "manliness." In *13 Moons*, Elvira is beaten up by such a specimen while cruising for sex in men's clothes. When she meets him again later on, she warns Rote Zora, who replies in cheeky defiance, "I fancy him anyway!"

made him into a model exemplifying a development away from cruel rigidity toward a more feeling position. He also made him face the basic question of every hysteric: Am I a man or am I a woman? And what does it mean to be a man?

But Biberkopf's body has already produced the answers: his delusions, bouts of depression, and physical reactions are full-blown rebellions. On this level, what his mind has been unable to grasp, his body has already processed. A truth has been forced upon him that is ineluctable and hard to accept: that things can't go on like this, that his claims are illusory, that his personal power has its limits. All he must do now is recognize that something is missing and that this is necessarily so. For a castration has already happened in any case: they really have lopped it off (leaving behind a vagina-like scar on the stump of his arm).

In *BA*/14, the process of acknowledgment reaches its peak. Biberkopf is positively forced to take further and final steps. Together with its main character, the film itself now becomes hallucinatory and enters a regressive phase (that is an abyss of cultural references). Reinhold whips Biberkopf with a petticoat, a bodybuilder hefts his weights in front of a sentimentally militaristic court painting from Germany around 1900 (an officer hands some significant object to his kneeling subordinate). Cilly, full of contempt: "Snarl! It's hardly worth it with that man. The guy's not up to very much: there's no meat and no fat on him." Reinhold kneels on a prayer stool ("Gaze aloft, the saving eyes see you all, such tender penitents," from Mahler's Eighth Symphony, after Goethe's *Faust II*). Biberkopf slurps food from a tin plate on the floor, encircled by rats (Janis Joplin, "Me and Bobby McGee"; Kraftwerk, "Radioactivity"). He is not comfortable in his human body and wants to become an animal: "Run across the fields … and the wind blows." His new friends, the rats, scratch a hole in the brick wall. Behind it, Reinhold and Mieze are making out in a Salvation Army room (Velvet Underground, "Candy Says"). From here, Biberkopf wanders into a chapel and finds himself in the forest again. He digs at the soil and in the resulting hole he sees Cilly in a room with blood-spattered tiles singing Schubert's "Death and the Maiden" and plunging a knife into her body again and again.

Antagonistic feelings—need and surfeit, aggression and longing for love—are pushed to extremes and right up close. On a street at night, the location of the car accident in *BA*/6, there is now a stage. While Willy plays piano, Cilly sings another song, and soldiers march through the picture, Biberkopf and Eva lie together in front of a car. She breastfeeds him before getting up and sitting down at the wheel. Biberkopf leans over the hood and retches up his liquid meal. Competing demands are rendered with a similar degree of compression (going beyond Döblin here, too) in the final confrontation between Biberkopf and Reinhold. At the end of a public boxing match, Biberkopf walks across to his adversary and kisses him on the mouth.

Relief

This grand parade of phantasms is not only of personal significance; Biberkopf's penitence is also credited with more general relevance. After all, the mechanisms of repression and displacement function similarly on a societal level: painful memories are avoided, detours are made, symptoms produced. Consequently, the type of neurosis represented by Biberkopf continues to define the frame for these events. What Freud said about hysterical symptoms applies: they symbolize memory fragments, they are substitutes, they repeat traumatic experiences, and they displace acute sexual wishes from childhood into the production of compromises.[19] But now, the place of these repressed wishes that insist on returning is assigned to specific aspects of German history. In Döblin's version, phantasms are already accumulating in the form of militaristic aggressiveness, giving Biberkopf's mindset a shrill, nationalistic undertone. In this way, Döblin highlighted a culture hardened and rendered unwholesome by the experience of World War I. In Fassbinder's version, its place is taken by "National Socialism," "World War II," and "concentration camp" (as a manmade real).

As a result, the action in *BA*/14 keeps switching to a set of rooms that bear a striking resemblance to a scene of German mass murder. In an abattoir, a mound of dying, naked bodies lies in a tiled corner. Biberkopf moves toward the pile, undresses, and lies down with the others. Reinhold appears and swings an ax through the mountain of meat. In the next shot, Biberkopf is lying on a dissecting table where Reinhold prepares him like a sacrificial animal. Then, in one of the last, especially theatrical scenes, Biberkopf becomes the "Christ Child" and is nailed to the cross—against a back projection of Hieronymus Bosch's *Garden of Earthly Delights* and an atomic bomb that detonates at the moment of his death. And then this room also contains the heaviest symbol of all: a furnace of the kind used at concentration camps.

From the angels' perspective, these events look different again. To them, wars and revolutions possess more or less the same degree of futility. What they see, as the net result of all the terror and fervor, is only the trail of blood they leave behind. Elated, even cheerful, Sarug and Terah clear away the

19 As listed by Freud in "Hysterical Fancies and Their Relations to Bisexuality" (1908), in Sigmund Freud, *Selected Papers on Hysteria and Other Psychoneuroses* (New York: Journal of Nervous and Mental Disease Publishing Company, 1912), 197–98.

war dead while making fun of missed historical opportunities and crushed hopes: "Rejoicing and shouting. Marching six abreast, two or three abreast: so marches the French Revolution, so the Russian Revolution; the Peasants' Wars, the Anabaptists. They all march behind Death. There is rejoicing in his wake. Onward to freedom! To freedom! The old world must fall, wake up, morning air, rrrum-ti-tum! Brothers, onward to the sun, to freedom, brothers, to the light above! In sixes, twos, and threes. Brothers, to the sun, to freedom, to the light above. The future shines brightly out of the dark past. Forward march, right, left, left, right. Rrrum-ti-tum!"

Mountains of corpses and cremation furnaces, obliteration by fire, lives turned to dust, a cycle of immutabilities, desire for (self-)annihilation, major transformation via sacrifice, the bloodbath as the primal scene of all lawmaking and civilization: this really can be called a grim and dubious setting, and not just because of the way it corresponds to the etymology of the now nonetheless commonly used word "Holocaust."

Does this mean that Fassbinder trivialized the monstrosities of recent German history? This is a possible view, but it is not one I share. Besides the fact that the film *BA* is one of the few German responses that cut to the quick, any "political" assessment of its attempts at historicization should rather focus on the historical perspectives it established. In 1929, World War I was the recent past and National Socialism lay in the immediate future. Similarly, World War II and the Holocaust were the past for the Federal Republic of Germany in 1980. At that time, people had a dark vision of the future. In accordance with widespread assumptions, Fassbinder's films after 1977 repeatedly broadcast the slogan: "Fascism will triumph."

Fascism is always one possible future, of course. But in view of the way *BA* is devised, such a prophecy also appears almost glib. It is blocked, for example, by a model of time that recalls the psychoanalytic concept of memory. For Freud, regression takes place when a current image becomes associated with earlier, unconscious content. This motion is not equivalent to a reconstruction of some past, but rather utilizes old material to invent, construct, layer, and rearrange new images that make an impact in the present.

What holds for a subject does not apply in exactly the same way for a narrative, but it is not entirely incomparable. Fassbinder's regressive movement is linked back to a text that contains a potential, something with a future; something open to a renewed working through. This allowed him to find motifs in this text even for far weightier analogies that went beyond the temporal frame of Döblin's *BA*.

It is not even certain, however, that the Holocaust really does play a central (or virtual) part in *BA*, as claimed above. Although there is reason enough to sustain and integrate memories of this part of German history, and even if this weighty motif remains *the* object of memory, it is possible that this in turn conceals something else. If this were the case, it would be a proxy within a reworking in which other, more currently repressed motifs are hidden.

"Forward, Sisters and Brothers, Onward to the Sun"

There are, after all, sufficient reasons to elide shocks and injuries. Fassbinder's key intervention, referred to here as "hystericizing," consists of paving a way out of the defensive position for these shocks. *BA* was supposed to be like a school where one could learn how to affirm the emotions and idiosyncrasies one has anyway and to render them legible. Whereas neuroses seek to undo something that has happened in the past, the aim here was to interrupt sterile cycles, to set something in motion, to become tender, to relent, to open up to things, to create a capacity for love, and to surrender one's fear.

The hysteric is no radiant figure of freedom, however. He is deficient, and he lives in genuine agony. Yet his symptoms have already reacted to what is hard to assimilate. While compulsive obsessive neurosis shifts affect intensities from a traumatizing event to a marginal or harmless image, hysteria transforms them into somatic energy and assigns it to particular body parts. Hysteria as a type of affliction thus becomes a model for the portrayal of aporias. Something opens up so that something else can be closed. Something is transgressed and not transgressed. Unlike the pervert, who adequately comes to terms with his symptom, the hysteric suffers. Unlike the obsessive, who locks everything up in his stingy and aggressive no, the hysteric at least produces the ambiguity of a yes-and-no. "Hystericization" is not a solution for good endings; here, too, exchanges and transactions are mere ersatz. To Fassbinder's mind, it was better to suffer from something than not to suffer at all; to no longer immediately wish the irksome other person dead would be a start.

Achieving even this is difficult enough. Added to which, the path is blocked by the obsessives, who are at an advantage if only because they have common sense on their side. They have already clenched their butts, brought everything under control, and thus have no reason to shake anything up. Lacan often described this position in harsh terms: "The obsessive drags into the cage of his narcissism the objects in which his question reverberates in the multiplied alibi of deadly figures and, mastering their high-wire act, addresses his ambiguous homage toward the box in which he himself has his seat, that of the master who cannot be seen."[20]

Artistic production is not immune to this approach. At present, many artists and writers actually tend toward this

20 Jacques Lacan, *Écrits*, trans. Bruce Fink (New York: Norton, 2006), 250.

obsessive type, often the most successful. Even the most assiduous realistic storytelling is spiced with trivial complexity: distancing techniques, monologues, "affectionate observation," erudite references, treatments of history in the past tense, the minor dramas of personal derangement, exploration of "roots" and "identities," and now also satire and "self-irony." One possible explanation: the future is blocked off, "we are living in post-apocalyptic times."[21] This results in another persistent feature that Alain Badiou once found disconcerting—the way that "no one gets involved any more with the political creation of a new man. On the contrary, what we hear from all sides is the demand for the conservation of the old humanity."[22]

This was not how things were meant to be in *BA*. Fassbinder did not want to confirm "what I really am"; he was more interested in what "I will have been." In this light, the process triggered in his film was supposed to be like a psychoanalytic cure. Along with Biberkopf, Fassbinder wanted to put the viewer (and the whole of Germany) on the couch—in a fifteen-hour televised session with no hope of success or proposed solution.[23]

In spite of this, at the end of the suffering sequence in *BA*/14 the narrator reports an accomplishment: "Let us extol what the pain does to Franz Biberkopf. Let us speak of the destruction pain causes. Breaking off, cutting down, casting down, disin-

21 As Jack Donaghy (Alec Baldwin) put it in episode 3 of season 5 of the TV show *30 Rock*.

22 Alain Badiou, *The Century*, trans. Alberto Toscano (Cambridge, MA: Polity, 2007), 20–21.

23 A question in the interview by Limmer/Rumler (1980) tried once again to simply offload this onto the author as a person: "So is it therapy when RWF shoots films?" Answer: "There's always an element of therapy, sure. But there is always also an attempt to gain a slightly better understanding of part of myself—anything. It's not therapy via a third figure, like in psychoanalysis. Instead, it's therapy via the work." Fischer, *Fassbinder über Fassbinder*, 507.

tegrating: that's what it does." And the voice adds: "At this evening hour, Franz Biberkopf died, former transport worker. … Another man lay in the bed in which he had lain. The other man has the same papers as Franz; he looks like Franz; but in another world he has another name."

Biberkopf has traversed the most extreme emotional states and agonizingly overcome the forces of inertia. Now he has accomplished a change of position; under a new name (Franz Karl) he has reached a higher stage of existence. He is supposed to have emerged from his conflicts and traumas a stronger person, to have learned to face fundamental helplessness and the reality of death, to have reined in his childish and obsessive demands and thus come a step closer to the truth of his desire. The therapy is now over, then; he has survived it, things have calmed down. Fittingly, he now works amid the immobile traffic of a garage.

For Döblin, this change of position achieved and portrayed by means of hallucinogesis amounted to a "healing." [Tales of a Long Night] Biberkopf is credited with an ability to be part of a community. He is supposed to have become someone capable of solidarity, perhaps a socialist, who freely bends to the needs of a collective under the condition of participating in something that can be realized neither through him nor without him.[24]

In spite of the tendency toward irresistible contradictions then, this opens up a space of freedom and potential change in *BA*. For Fassbinder, the question of how to live together was a central one. He nonetheless modified Döblin's notion of a "solution" in a crucial way. In the film we hear that "it's nicer

24 This already struck Döblin's contemporaries as weird and implausible. To Walter Benjamin, for example, this reversal seemed like "the most extreme and most vertiginous, the last and most advanced stage of the old bourgeois *Bildungsroman*." Benjamin, "Crisis of the Novel," 304.

and better to be with others." And in the debate on participation in *BA*/13, Fassbinder gave special emphasis to such wishes: "Why should we all work for one guy? On the other hand, in my opinion, a genuine collaboration would be the finest thing of all." But ultimately, these sentiments were outweighed by his skepticism. Whether and how such far-reaching changes might filter through into society is left open. For one thing, even in the manageable framework of small groups, productive conditions are rarely created.[25] And for another, there is no shortage of potential for false identification (family, nation, gender, religion).

As a result, the end approaches amid maximum ambiguity. In the original script, the final episode bore the title "On the Death of a Child and the Birth of Someone Useful." The "rare misfortune" of growing up had already shown itself to be contradictory. This spirit is maintained until the final credits, over which a stupefying acoustic chaos is performed. Its most clearly audible elements are two recordings that must have sounded similarly outdated and oppressive in 1980: the Socialist "Internationale" ("Forward, brothers and sisters, the last fight let us face!") and the National Socialist "Horst Wessel Song" ("The flag on high! Ranks tightly closed!"). Both point to paths that are no longer viable. With reference to Biberkopf this is meant to tell us: this rebirth or resurrection could be as a fascist; his opening up to his fellow human beings could lead straight into the arms of a community defined along "racial" lines. Or not, since steps can be taken or not taken.

25 Film productions, too, are forms of living within particular power structures. In the early 1970s, Fassbinder often expressed disappointment concerning his experiences in this area: "All I know is that Willi [Peer Raben] and myself had a strong reason and desire to work in a group, and that we also had the wish not always to be the leader of the group. And there was always a striving to activate the others, but it was difficult"; "It really is incredibly depressing that this unique vitality came to nothing"; "At the time it was a group; today I know that it wasn't one." Interview with Corinna Brocher (1973), in Fischer, *Fassbinder über Fassbinder*, 90, 75, 164.

Many grand last words are spoken in *BA*, but the best and the most mysterious come right at the close. Here, ontological oneness is confronted with a diametrically opposed utopia. The narrator announces: "He's an assistant gatekeeper in a factory. What kind of fate is that? Immediately after the trial, Biberkopf is offered a job as an assistant gatekeeper in a factory. He accepts it. There is nothing further to report about his life here. One may be stronger than I am. When we are two, it's more difficult to be stronger than I am. If there are ten of us, even more difficult. If there are a thousand of us or a million, then it's really difficult. But it's also nicer and better to be with others. Then I sense and know everything much more certainly. A ship is not firmly moored without a big anchor, and a man cannot exist without many other people. What is true and what is false … I shall know better now. … Be alert! There's something going on in the world. All is not sweet in the world." Biberkopf adds (in voice-over): "If they drop gas bombs, I'll suffocate. No one knows why they dropped them, but you don't have to know. There was time to take care of things like that." The narrator, Fassbinder's voice, counters: "If there's a war, and they draft him, though he doesn't know why, and the war goes on anyway, then that's his fault; and it serves him right. Be alert! Be alert! One is not alone. Hail and rain may fall from the sky. There's nothing you can do about it; but about a lot of other things you can. He won't shout as he used to do: 'It's fate, fate!' You don't have to revere it as fate. You must look it in the face, grasp it."

In 1929, this was already out of step with Benjamin's "voracious fate," with Schmitt's friend/foe divide as the fundamental definition of the political, and with Brecht's call for art to generate partisanship.

Ambiguity shapes the entire picture here. In fact, Fassbinder's *BA* shows what an ambiguous thing a cinematic picture is.

Arc de cercle

> Do you think the form of our productions suits their political purpose?
> —From a questionnaire handed out by Brecht after a performance of *The Decision*

> In my opinion, it's really a film the audience won't have an easy time with, but actually quite a hard one.
> —Fassbinder on *Love Is Colder Than Death*

In the preceding chapters I have often mentioned Bertolt Brecht, largely due to the great influence still exerted in 1970s West Germany by his politicized definition of the function of art. It may not appear so at first glance, but Fassbinder's approach was not entirely irreconcilable with this. He too wanted to shape tastes, devise modern forms of grace, and make his work as naive as possible, with the quality of a ballad. Like Brecht, he used traditional forms, old idioms, and historical materials to develop a demotic, even folksy artificiality, deploying the latest technologies and transgressing media borders.[1] But Fassbinder did not share Brecht's belief in the emancipatory powers of media didacticism and aesthetic dissociation of given aesthetic elements. In Fassbinder's version, enlightenment started from an entirely different point, based on the application

1 Fassbinder approached Brecht indirectly via Marieluise Fleißer and her play *Pioneers in Ingolstadt* (1928). Fleißer was a good choice for other reasons, too: as well as sharing her keen eye for the details of bourgeois power structures, Fassbinder must also have liked the openly interested gaze she directed at men with attractive, muscular bodies. He may also have appreciated certain aspects of her biography: a brief stint as the "it" girl of

of psychoanalytic reason. Under such conditions, calls for a change of position or "freeing humanity from its immaturity" took a different shape.

For Fassbinder, a meaningful political position for artistic work included an inquiry into emotions and all the forms through which drives manifest themselves. (As a result, he also created a significant erotic oeuvre.) He took these bodily responses seriously as projections of historical calamities and societal miseries. Since the emotions are also an indicator essentially accessible to all, he aimed to amplify them and take them to the outer limit of the capacity for suffering. This, in essence, was his program.

For a while, Sirkian melodrama did possess special (though not exclusive) relevance as a possible mode of presentation. Its suitability as a model was due, among other things, to its ability to act out predicaments and contradictions, doing so within the framework of mass-cultural address and with international reach.[2]

Fassbinder aimed for a form of kitsch that is not mindless, patronizing, smarmy, or overwhelming, but whose simplifications are based instead on the greatest sensitivity, intelligence,

avant-garde theater; eclectic choices of partner; drifting, after a brief liaison with Brecht, into ultra-right-wing milieus; asking, in 1931, for "Jewish" press blurbs to be removed from the cover of her latest book (including one by Walter Benjamin, the only sympathetic one); member of the Nazi "Reich Chamber of Culture." Fleißer left behind a body of work kept slender by scruples. Since the late 1960s, her plays have once more been staged by left-wing theater groups.

2 Fassbinder in an interview with Christian Brad Thomsen (1971): "American cinema is the only one I can really take seriously because it actually reaches its audience. German cinema before 1933 achieved this, too, and of course there are some directors in other countries who are in touch with the audience." Fischer, *Fassbinder über Fassbinder*, 221. "We just aren't as naive as Raoul Walsh or Howard Hawks or whoever. Instead, in everything we do, we always have to think why we're doing it. But I'm sure that one day I'll be able to tell naive stories." Interview with Christian Brad Thomsen (1972), in ibid., 235.

and scrupulousness. Within this approach, the wishes, longings, and sentimentalities, the circular wisdom of tautologies, the reflections in the mirror, and the deeply illusionary character of "filmic" expression were a necessary condition.[3] But to become a source of real power, the scene had to be more broadly focused. For although Fassbinder's films were meant to be "beautiful," he also wanted them to give the audience a hard time. Ingrid Caven: "We wanted to work on style; we were concerned with the aesthetic. We wanted to learn something, to entertain, and to give beauty." This made it necessary to engage with profoundly aporetic structures. Only then was it possible to prevent the narrative from descending into illustration, representation, and pure everydayness, providing it instead with tension, urgency, and brutality, without which the result would be just "a kind of naturalism that is no longer compatible with the demands of art."[4]

As well as "giving beauty," this fuller mode of articulation stages the kind of games that attempt to assimilate what is most unpleasant and incomprehensible within a differential logic. But something uncanny also looms in Fassbinder's films, something that, like death, can destroy petty illusions and overarching structures at any time, spawning disconcertment, fear, and terror.

The prestige of the political in art does not normally depend on such complexities, with indignant reactions to current affairs usually being quite sufficient. But if a fiction learns to navigate such increased complexity, it can be truer than

3 Interview with Corinna Brocher (1973): "The only thing that was tried in the case of *Rio das Mortes*, that I tried, was that I said I wanted to try not to make films that have bad taste" (ibid., 61). "And then: it should also be beautiful" (interview with Joachim von Mengershausen, 1969, in ibid., 183).

4 Interview with Brocher (1973), in ibid., 148.

what actually exists, allowing even a movie to attain something like realism. This in turn makes it possible to tell the truth through lying images and words. When Godard said film is twenty-four frames of truth per second, he may have coined a cute modernist *bon mot.* But Fassbinder's rejoinder came closer to the way things are: film is twenty-five lies per second.[5]

Film narrative assembles different kinds of enunciation into a fabric. They are only effective when they grab the viewer, when they "do" something, make something happen, or set something in motion. Fassbinder's "interventionism" and his assumptions about the political in artistic productions were based on what might be called a therapeutic principle. Since there can be no self-analysis, a film was to take the place of the other person. The viewer would receive his or her own message from the film, or perhaps an inverted version of that message. Transferences can fail, however. Or, sadder still, remain without consequences.[6]

Berlin Alexanderplatz was also a test. Completed just in time for the 102nd birthday of hysteria, Fassbinder had updated a surrealist notion of politics. The series was his attempt to build a school of desire and dreaming, and to foster a different logic, a different poetry, and a work of love, on television. Sometimes it takes time to understand, but then even stones can cry.

5 Quoted in "Schütte: Von der Dialektik des Bürgers im Paradies der lähmenden Ordnung," in Rainer Werner Fassbinder, *Filme befreien den Kopf: Essays und Arbeitsnotizen*, ed. Michael Töteberg (Frankfurt am Main: Fischer, 1984), 130.

6 "After the premiere of the first two episodes on television, I actually received death threats. In Cologne there is an officially recognized association called 'The Society for the Preservation of the Cleanness and Purity of Germany' and I actually received death threats from them." Interview with Georges Bensoussan (1981), in Fischer, *Fassbinder über Fassbinder*, 563. "I am utterly bewildered by this, because I think that *Alexanderplatz*, apart from episode fourteen—or the 'Epilog' as it's now called—is incredibly beautiful,

interesting and eye-opening, and actually not at all suited to provoking aggression against itself. That has always been how I saw *Alexanderplatz*. I was expecting discussions, I was even hoping for them. But as things stand at the moment, the aggression is directed toward the series itself. [...] All I can say now is that it's beyond belief." Interview with Limmer/Rumler (1980), in ibid., 507–8.

Supplements

Berlin, Super-City

A fascination with the effects of a capitalist dynamic was omnipresent in the "city novels" of the 1920s, but it also served to emphasize the authors' own modernity. Carl Van Vechten's novel *Parties* (1930) offers a typical example:

> New York is in a constant state of mutation. [...] Leave town for a week and you will notice changes when you return. It is quite possible to pay a visit to your lawyer or your bank only to discover that the erstwhile building in which their business was formerly transacted has disappeared in favor of a deep hole in the ground. Contrariwise, a new and glittering tower, fifty or more stories in height, may rise in another direction before you are aware of the preparatory excavations. It is quite possible in New York to lease an apartment on the thirty-fourth floor with a splendid and uninterrupted view and a great deal of sunlight only to find before a year has passed that both view and sunlight have been blocked out by a taller neighbor.[1]

Those who read Döblin's novel today, or who know it only from hearsay, often assume it contains or deals with this kind of modernity. If the reader in question actually lives in Berlin's Mitte district, he or she may even feel prompted to compare the current scene with that preserved in the novel, engaging in a little retrospective local sociology. The first insight resulting from any such study is that the area to the

1 Carl Van Vechten, *Parties: Scenes from Contemporary New York Life* (New York: A. A. Knopf, 1930), 154.

northwest of Alexanderplatz where *BA* is set has changed a great deal. Today, the neighborhood formerly known as the "Scheunenviertel," once inhabited by petty criminals and poor Jewish immigrants from Eastern Europe, is quiet and boutiquey, an upscale residential district, and a destination for mass youth tourism.

Whichever form such interest in big cities takes, what is astonishing is its staying power. Whether it's theories about nightlife, urban sociology, or "metro zones," whether it's conceived of along the "conflict lines" of a capitalist or "postcapitalist" "logic of the production of space," or devoted to "labor in the metropolis" (Antonio Negri), a kind of overall view always seems to prevail, leading to old metaphors of the urban and thus to false generalizations.

Where Berlin is concerned, the fascination of the big city took on completely different associations after World War II. At a stroke, the city felt old and gray. Berlin became a museum of its former selves, whose ruins and vacant lots could now be charged with wistful innuendo. Reunification put an end to this; today, that Berlin has been completely built over or thoroughly renovated. One striking aspect of this process was the ease with which the diverse avant-garde architectural traditions on which the city had so prided itself could be ignored in the name of "critical reconstruction" when it came to the need to erect large numbers of new representative buildings. After 1990, demand focused exclusively on bone-dry, low-budget monumentality in highly pompous forms. Since then, there has been a shift in attitudes: "If things don't change soon, the city will become one giant gravestone" (*Süddeutsche Zeitung*, December 6, 2010). Significantly, the already much-reduced interest in architecture has now been almost entirely redirected toward a full reconstruction of the Hohenzollern palace leveled in

1950. In spite of the way a "legacy" has been imagined here where there is nothing to inherit, it is clear that historico-political gestures and the aestheticization of claims to power have been harnessed to the cause of remedying supposed shortfalls in national prestige.

"The palace was not in Berlin—Berlin was the palace" (*Frankfurter Allgemeine Zeitung*). And because, traditionally, the *FAZ* knows best "what Germany needs," the highbrow newspaper also knew the following: not just a particular cultural policy, but the place itself "calls for a palace." This intellectual confusion about one throwback easily becomes the basis for others. Patrick Bahners: "When the state can afford to allow beauty to come into its own [we are still talking about the palace], then it is a pleasure to be a German citizen" (*FAZ*, July 6, 2007). Of course, the new German citizen of pleasure doesn't actually require another palace in Berlin in order to feel ties with achievements and a national culture—but how pleasant it is nonetheless to casually adopt positions in one's own interest, to generate meaning, and to define urban spaces. After all, the same approach is also taken by artists, who, according to Berlin's recent mythology, play a crucial role on another level ("city of artists," "Berlin as a cultural laboratory"). "Berlin is a super-city. This is not actually anything new, but word seems to be getting round. Above all, of course, among 'creatives' of every stripe" (*die tageszeitung*, May 4, 2007). Likewise in the PR of art institutions: "The German capital changes continually, remaining fragmentary, diverse, and contradictory. This wealth of contrasts coupled with a relaxed mood is attractive, not only to artists from around the world" (6th Berlin Biennale, 2010). Of course, this leads to further conclusions: "After 1945, this state transformed itself into a model liberal polity" (Josef Joffe, on the possible use of the Bendlerblock, where the failed assassination attempt on Hitler in July 1944 was planned and where those responsible were executed, as a set for the film *Valkyrie*, in the weekly newspaper *Die Zeit*, July 5, 2007). In the left-wing *tageszeitung*, this model character is often seen in similar terms, but with a slightly different slant; here, it is "1968," the rise of the Green Party, "civil society," and even the *tageszeitung* itself that are said to have "thoroughly civilized Germany."

Döblin's novel is not open to insights of this kind, not least because his view of the city's flourishing under capitalism was far more profound in every way. In one respect, however, his choice of location was clairvoyant. To this day, Alexanderplatz has remained the windswept, unattractive, and eternally provisional point of transit it already was at the time, as Piel Jutzi's film adaptation of *BA* from 1931 clearly shows.

The specific form taken on by an imaginary Berlin in Fassbinder's film—here the intermediate level of a subway station, there a street corner with a double-decker bus and a few old cars, basically whatever secondhand sets were available at Bavaria Film Studios in Munich—provided the bare minimum of local color and symbols of urban hustle and bustle required for a production of this magnitude.

German Calamities (1980–2010)

> To see what we can achieve and, as a result, to gain a better picture of ourselves.
> —Angela Merkel, 2009

An entirely different story must be added here. It constitutes the pragmatic and in every way negative reverse of what interests me about Fassbinder's films, but it is nonetheless related: the systematic shifts in German cinema around 1980 and their (ongoing) impact on cinematic representations of the German present and past.

Around 1977, producers and industry-affiliated publications set about breaking "the fatal power of the film directors" and retaking the cultural high ground from auteur cinema. The whole thing had the character of a smear campaign and, over the years, became increasingly aggressive. Auteur movies were mocked as elitist, didactic, and dirigiste. Criticism was also leveled at the system of funding committees and TV editors, who were accused of enabling such films with a disregard for the public's tastes.[1] (Vocal critics in this vein included a certain Günter Rohrbach, who also regularly worked with Fassbinder.) Not all of these charges were unfounded. German auteur movies of this

1 In the period 1977/78, around sixty films were produced in West Germany, half of them by directors associated with the New German Cinema. A few significant titles: *The American Friend* (Wim Wenders), *Stroszek* (Werner Herzog), *Hitler: A Film from Germany* (Hans-Jürgen Syberberg), *The All-Round Reduced Personality: Redupers* (Helke Sander), *Beer Chase* (Herbert Achternbusch), *Flaming Hearts* (Walter Bockmayer), *The Left-Handed Woman* (Peter Handke), *The Second Awakening of Christa Klages* (Margarethe von Trotta), and *Despair* (Fassbinder).

period often really were dull, technically inexperienced, and had limited charisma. That most of them were also commercially unsuccessful was their Achilles' heel, the angle from which their other claims and qualities could be called into question (film as a medium of personal expression, criticism of its "misuse" as a commodity, pedagogical and emancipatory art praxis).[2]

Ultimately, however, the campaign was about funds and rerouting state subsidies into one's own pocket. Nonetheless, attempts were also made to harness the international repute of the New German Cinema to the cart of the conventional film industry with its newfound longing for international box-office hits.

But however professional German cinema wished to become, the results of these producers' dreams remained contrived and insipid. Germany quite simply lacked the necessary personnel, thematic resonance, and narrative capabilities for the creation of Hollywood imitations. Scriptwriting was identified as the main weak point here and generations of German film students were subsequently brought into line. At the film schools, countless rulebooks, mostly of American descent, disseminated their wisdom on

2 Film theorist Thomas Elsaesser studied the history of this critical reception in depth and affirmed some of its arguments. German auteur cinema of these years, he writes, really did go too far in its fetishization of outsiders and marginal groups, as well as, most importantly, failing to develop "mythical" echoes or viable models for addressing the audience. Elsaesser's central point was that the film subsidies introduced in West Germany in the 1960s and the Film-Television Agreement in 1974 enabled the West German film boom at the price of being "state-sanctioned art." In this way, he continues, the "cultural" became a substitute currency with the task of creating new forms of national identity. This "materialist" angle seems rather rancorous, not only with regard to Fassbinder's films. For one thing, any artistic boom is based on special economic conditions, and for another, there is little to be said against "state-sanctioned art" as long as it facilitates productions like *BA*. Elsaesser, *New German Cinema*, 8–9.

controlled emotional arcs in three acts, two conflicts, and one key trait per character, plus plot points positioned with split-second accuracy.

In any rate, there was to be no more "art," and lecturing was similarly rejected, with faith placed instead in lessons of the heart, as well as vehement claims of merely wanting to tell a neat little story. As subsequent years were to show, the results generated by this vocation to mass-produce quick gratification were clumsy, calculating, and drab on every level. Aesthetic, dramatic, or expressive effect was always pushed for at precisely the wrong point. The atmospheres were too flat or too garish, jokes didn't work, humor was stripped of every one of its functions, and even vulgarity became an entirely listless affair. Portrayals of concrete social contexts were certainly no longer on the agenda, and the extreme monotony and complete lack of variety finished off German cinema for good.

In a word, this cinema lacked everything that might have underpinned its own claims to mass compatibility. Unable to address an audience in the plural, or to credit it with a range of knowledge, desires, and demands (as many American productions have done, even those made for television), these films loudly championed the mature viewer only to mine the catalogue of idées reçues all the more insolently. Because their conformism had to be somehow compensated for, there were inflated claims of "grand cinema": "emotions," "courage," "cinema must be dangerous and passionate." Such hyperbole has been a staple of the PR for German films ever since.

This extremism of magnified emotions brought forth a "realism" whose ingratiating uncouthness reached all the way to the character constellations, acting styles, and planned emotional impact. Now, all of the characters were somehow equally confident, breathless, or pressured, the looks were all piercing, there was much shouting of lines. But however accomplished these poses of eruptive passion were considered to be, they never went beyond caricatures of method acting. Above all, this German cinema and television was now far more miserable, noxious, and reactionary than everything turned against by a group of German filmmakers in 1962 with their Oberhausen Manifesto.

But these normalizations were restricted neither to West Germany nor to the film industry. Not only had cinema in the United States taken a sharp turn toward the populist and the infantile since the early 1980s, but comparable developments were also seen in the field of art. Here, figurative painting had the role of offering more vigorous alternatives to the "intellectuality" and "coldness" of "conceptualism." In spite of similarly revisionist tendencies, however, Neo-Expressionism could at least permit itself an occasional "fuck you," using painting to show a lack of appetite for the "new appetite for painting."[3]

Such outbursts did not occur in the German cinema of the period. Using films to express a lack of appetite for the "love of cinema" would have been incompatible with the cure-all cinephilia that attempted to pin a badge of highbrow quality on even the most tedious productions. In particularly devious cases, the sentimentality, legibility, or pictorial quality that had been demanded from films since the early 1980s was tagged as "postmodern." Alternatively (but amounting

3 This reflects an interesting point in art sociology: Whereas in the 1960s, as I have claimed above, feature films became attractive to writers as a form of production, for the period after 1980 one can observe that in Germany certain intellectual and social profiles were no longer drawn to cinema in the same way. They likely turned to a different field, most probably the art world where, a decade later, it was becoming possible and even usual to work with audiovisual media. In the late 1970s, Martin Kippenberger was still interested in "going into cinema"—as an actor.

to more or less the same thing), movies were automatically categorized as pop simply because they were part of mass culture. While West German attempts to attain European standards of cinematic modernism in the 1960s made little headway (possibly for similar reasons), the postmodern phase was left out entirely. The list of discursive and politicizing waves that totally bypassed German cinema and television is endless.

All of this set the scene for the situation in which we still find ourselves. Not only have we never gotten away from the simply defined characters or the conflicts of families, relationships, and adolescence, but even the most boorish productions still lay claim to passions that supposedly go "straight to the heart." A brief look at television in Germany today is enough to see that the countless diligent nuns, good-natured hoteliers and horse breeders, priests and vintners, captains, senior physicians, police officers of all ranks, the "female executive spoiled by success," the "attractive and self-assured communications trainer," or the "stem-cell researcher in a crisis of meaning" are also signs of this society's seriously disturbed structures of cultural self-regulation. The far higher percentage of German films in cinemas and on television since the 1980s has contributed to accustoming audiences to such impoverishment of content, making it seem more or less insurmountable.

One may claim, then, that the "spiritual and moral turn" proclaimed by Helmut Kohl in 1982, so often accused of having come to nothing, was in fact highly successful. But this was especially true in the field of film and television, which has not undergone another wave of politicization since. Adorno's remark that the situation left behind in Germany by the Nazi State Music Bureau (Reichsmusikkammer) is comparable to a heap of rubble can thus be fittingly applied to the more recent developments described here.

How one defaces one's own present reality is one thing. But the situation becomes more critical, especially in Germany, when the subject matter in question is the past. Here, too, the shifts over the last three decades are quite clear. I do not wish to revisit all of the various milestones on the path to the kind of relaxed German nationalism that is now routinely evoked at every available occasion (visit to a cemetery with SS graves by Kohl and Reagan in 1985, the historians' dispute of 1986, Martin Walser's discovery of "historical feelings," racist attacks in the period after reunification); this would require a review of all the artistic developments since the late 1960s in theater, in literature, and in fine art, without which their subsequent impact on mass culture would not have been conceivable. Suffice it to say that Fassbinder, too, was involved in this development, as he dealt intensely with recent German history and its implications.

For Fassbinder, the calamity of the "German condition" was always something to be genealogized. In his "history films," he wanted to break through the vicious circle of a specifically German experience of prematurely abandoned or totally failed emancipations and revolutions (only ever realized—successfully for a time and, at that time, longed for by everyone—in the form of National Socialism).

Although Fassbinder exerted no artistic influence on German cinema to speak of, the constructions of the German "history films" of recent years almost seem to be the negative of his approach, in some cases with an uncanny overlapping of themes and motifs. But whereas Fassbinder always sampled primarily from the margins, recent German productions do the exact opposite. Women are replaced by men, the periphery by the center, specific social viewpoints by authoritarian ones. Whereas in *Lili Marleen* (1981) Fassbinder looked at National Socialism through the eyes of a careerist female singer, in 2004 it had to be the perspective of the greatest German of them all, in his saddest moment (*Downfall*). While in Fassbinder's film, Hitler was rendered invisible by a blinding nimbus (thus avoiding the need for "congenial" performances), here he was banished to a dark bunker deep underground, probably with the intention of saving him from his downfall forever. Whereas in *The Marriage of Maria Braun* (1979), the famous radio commentary on the 1954 World Cup Final was just the soundtrack to the fateful comeuppance of a postwar profiteer, in 2003 the same historical moment was turned into a whole film (*The Miracle of Bern*) and glorified as a moment of happiness for Germans after the war. Whereas in *The Third Generation* (1978), the Baader-Meinhof terrorists appeared as bourgeois clowns, helping to aggravate capitalism's technological means of applying pressure, in *The Baader-Meinhof Complex* (2008) they were angry rebels pursuing their deadly serious and most certainly world-famous adventures, doomed to failure. And whenever one thought that enough was enough, the next fatal moment in German history was already being dug up.

Nothing shows the restorative character of German society better than this type of film and television productions, and the now-customary conceptions of history play an outstanding role here. But they too are ultimately the result of a production system that boldly empowers itself while accelerating artistic deflation. A symptomatic figure here was the film producer Bernd Eichinger. Not only was he among those who benefited from the abovementioned revolt of producers against auteur cinema, but once in position, he then presented himself as the better auteur filmmaker. As well as the kind of "Eichinger film" that tries to provide adequate German equivalents for the great American myths, he also made an art of championing his projects with the verve of the rebel, dangerous thinker, and taboo breaker even in cases when all he was doing was filming a bestseller or blatantly fighting a rearguard action. During the propaganda battle over *Downfall*, he presented himself as a poacher in the most forbidden zones of the German unconscious, and he gave a paranoid emotional charge (distrust, outrage, indictment) to something that was clearly based on bureaucratic logic or a commercial ploy, as every child today knows that Hitler always sells.[4]

What is striking here however—and this is at odds with his claims to personal involvement—is how willingly his historicization subscribed to the distance of the past tense. In this context, obsessive attention to detail performed the function of assuring the credibility and objectivity of the cinematic reconstruction down to the last button on every outfit. Eichinger behaved as if his subject matter was carved in stone for all time, a story capable of telling itself (hence the importance attached to achieving striking resemblances between the actors and the historical figures they portrayed).

German cinema certainly doesn't have a monopoly on strange reconstructions of history,[5] but it is fair enough to be harsher in judging German productions, even those that

4 Bernd Eichinger started off producing New German Cinema projects such as Wim Wenders's *The Wrong Move* (1975) or Hans-Jürgen Syberberg's *Hitler: A Film from Germany* (1977). *Christiane F.* (1981) was an early hit. As a producer, Eichinger fantasized about German or European movie productions with Hollywood-like appeal and international circulation. He subsequently turned to adaptations of successful novels: *The Name of the Rose* (1986) and *Elementary Particles* (2006), among others. Other films, some of which he also cowrote and directed, took great care in providing a particular German resonance.

5 There is no shortage of peculiar historicizations in American cinema either. Most take the form of retroverse transfer of innovation, meaning that a specific past is interpreted from the viewpoint of social standards that have now been firmly achieved.

don't fail (as so many do) to openly state their interests in the present. It makes a difference whether, firstly, I claim to tell a story "as it really was," allegedly cut off from the present, or, secondly, if I reconstruct the past due to a nostalgic need in the present, or, thirdly, and this is the rarest case, if I construct history to assemble a picture not of the past but of the present.

One might think that all these reminders of Nazism and the greatest trauma of recent German history should cause the greatest unease in German viewers. But insisting with such striking menace and pomposity on endless rehashing seems to have the opposite effect. So what is it then that gives pleasure here? Perhaps this: one is allowed, again and again, to imagine the situation before today's situation; i.e., the moment when the great German adventure of the twentieth century forced its way to the focal point of history, when the whole world held its breath, when the outcome was on

In Gus van Sant's *Milk* (2008), it was possible to film the life story of Harvey Milk—including all of the various attributes of "identity politics": pride, self-empowerment, struggling for a "we"—not least because today gay politicians are no longer inconceivable. Todd Haynes's *Far from Heaven* (2002) appropriated Sirkian melodrama in light of its feminist (1970s) and queer (1980s, 1990s) academic readings as a belated and rather blasé art exercise: now the husband really was as gay as the actor Rock Hudson was never permitted to be, although he could be today. In Ang Lee's *Brokeback Mountain* (2005) too, the reason for the ordeal, however powerfully portrayed, no longer exists in comparable severity. Such historicizations also exist in numerous "straight" versions. In the seven seasons of the television series *Mad Men* (2007–15), the New York of the advertising world from the 1960s onward is portrayed as a hell of petit-bourgeois etiquette and decorum. The breakdown of these codes is now widely taken for granted, but here they still provide melancholy appeal, as well as generating erotic stimuli. In *Deadwood* (2004–06), the portrayal of extreme misogyny becomes possible among other things because it can shrug off contemporary concerns by referring to the conditions prevailing in South Dakota in the late 1870s, while the strongest verbal profanities are nonetheless taken from the present ("cocksucker," "stupid cunt"). All of these films and series are driven by a similar longing that shows itself in the almost excessive care lavished on props and costumes—and it is almost as if repression itself is being offered up for enjoyment.

a knife-edge, hanging by a thread—when everything could have turned out quite differently.

This does not necessarily reflect an inability to get over losing the status of a major power. Nor must its revisionist logic necessarily attain the level of relativization reached during the historians' dispute (expansion of the definition of victimhood, the Holocaust explained in terms of prior genocides or as a "normal" act of war against "the Jews" as a political subject on the world stage). Nonetheless, it is surely no coincidence that German film and television audiences are so partial to being transported back to the most aggressive, illiberal, anti-emancipatory chapters of their country's history (or, with similar emphasis, to a devaluation of that history's more left-wing episodes: "1968," the entire GDR complex, etc.).

A noticeable impact also seems to have been made here by the altered geopolitical conditions after 1990, which clearly opened up new fields of activity for Germany as a "peaceful power" and "nation in self-imposed shackles" (expansive foreign policy; fanning ethnic and minority conflicts; aggressive militarization, step by step, including as a means of securing raw material resources and foreign trade; later also national trauma aftercare as a commodity for export).

This latent self-importance has also rubbed off on German narrative cinema. It shapes overall moods, but can also be identified in specifics—including the abovementioned proneness to overwrought forms of expression. Strangely, apart from inadequate acting styles, these improprieties manifest themselves above all on the level of visual design. Today, a conspicuously strong emphasis is placed on this aspect in German filmmaking, with almost every film for television now giving itself an arty color palette, using predominantly washed-out tones.

Even in films whose directors cannot be suspected of any direct involvement in the historical circumstances described here, the visual showing-off is unmistakable. One example here would be Tom Tykwer, who has always explained his vacuously pompous pictorialism in terms of "cinephilia." It may be that these forms of diligent emptiness lacking charm, suspense, and succinctness in fact hallucinate forms of empowerment that go beyond the realm of the cinema. Perhaps claims are being mulled over here that have yet to identify (let alone elaborate on) their genuine fields and targets.

The tendency toward anodyne iconophilia can also be observed in the minimalist counterpositions adopted in recent years by younger, more marginal filmmakers. Whereas big-budget German movies and television productions make compulsive and often primitive attempts to touch the audience with dramatic gimmicks, here diligence, emphatic distancing gestures, and a lack of tension are considered virtues. But this too launches an imaginary that supplies a post-Wall Germany with peculiar aestheticizations and questionable identity constructs.

I am referring here to films of what is sometimes called the "Berlin School," as well as stylistically related productions.[6] Their most striking characteristic: a renewed emphasis on the position of the auteur and a discourse of cinephile urgency. The filmmakers in question love cinema, they believe in cinema, and their aesthetic assumptions are once more couched in ethical and programmatic terms. They credit themselves with particularly close ties to all things real, or at least

6 To point to single movies, which are often underfinanced and independently produced, seems random and unfair, as innumerable German TV movies, to this very day, also share similar traits. Instead of a comprehensive list of titles I refer to MoMA's "The Berlin School: Films from the Berliner Schule," a program of a good dozen films screened at the end of 2013.

believe in their talent for "precise observation." Much is also made of the "picture," which is once again credited with precision, "magic," or even more mysterious qualities, perhaps even lessons in seeing. But while these directors (most of them men) pretend to be low-budget saviors of reality in the spirit of Kracauer or Bazin, they have merely carved out a more or less comfortable place for themselves in cool, swaggering cinematographic elegance. Although their notions of purity and transparency are schooled in the European cinema of the 1960s and '70s, they are adopted more on the basis of appearances and translated into a kind of style resembling New Objectivity.[7]

But this scholastic urge also displays all the limitations associated with "academism": nostalgic historicism, incorporeal opacity, bureaucratic production of meaning, sanctimonious aestheticism, avoidance of humor and turbulence.

This has a shaping influence on the films' narrative stance, atmospheres, and, not least, choice of characters. Despite claims to operate "on a level" with these figures, the results offer little evidence of genuine contact. Unlike a specific type of French cinema whose milieu portrayals can be socio-

7 Minimalist lethargy is not a purely German phenomenon, having been ubiquitous in international art-house cinema since the 1990s. But still, the German versions are always somehow more sluggish, solemn, and grueling. One remarkable exception in the European context is Lars von Trier. For a long time he too pursued a school-based agenda, while largely eschewing the need for assurance by cinematic essentialisms. In his work, postwar European cinematic modernism casts its shadow more in the form of perplexity. This is a reaction to the fact that feature films can no longer even hope for any social relevance or impact. A rebel as a matter of principle, von Trier's response to this lack of consequence often took the form of programmatic irony. Whereas many German films take place on an imaginary level, everything in von Trier's work is purely symbolic. The former knows no surplus, the latter no gaps. Even von Trier's irony cannot conceal the fact that his games are all controlled by a legislative and apodictic impulse, and a tendency to repressiveness. Despite their reactionary aroma, however, these films are never as deadly boring as most German ones.

logically quite precise, and that serves as a model for some of the German films in question, the portrayals offered by the "Berlin School" are woolly, the characters bland, and a diversity of human types is nowhere to be found.

Instead, a mood of graceful, vague alienation and melancholic intimacy is cultivated. Taciturnity, glum faces, and searching gazes are the predominant modes of expression. The characters, imprisoned in their own elegance, are treated with such lenience that their inviolability appears to be the actual subject matter. The focus here is on minor human entanglements, whose indestructible illusions are handled all the more carefully for being shared with those doing the handling.[8] The claim to a special sensitivity on the part of the German middle class thus becomes the sole room for maneuver in a school of storytelling that nonetheless passes for a "diagnostic view" of society.

All of this requires the addressee to identify with these "beautiful souls" and forms of completely nonspecific skepticism. Under conditions of enforced cinematic cultivation, one is expected to imagine oneself as an aesthete of one's own existence. Were one to submit to this, then nothing would remain (beyond this specific sensitivity) that might lay claim to any validity whatsoever.

Of course, even such an approach reproduces notions of the subject and of history. But its core may consist of mixed feelings similar to those dealt with more bluntly and brazenly by populist films that are less roundabout with their historical subject matter. Maybe these younger German melancholics too mourn not only a lack of participation in

8 Remarkable here are the retarded portrayals of sex and gender—not only in the eminently suited coming-of-age films that were quite popular for a while, which show adolescents as disgruntled little citizens-in-the-making.

society (which they do not want anyway) but also losses that took place on more distant fronts.

In other words, the flipside of all this might be the politically relevant dimension of this specifically German moroseness. If this were the case, then these enunciations that often seem so empty, prompting even *Cahiers du cinéma* to attribute a phantom quality to some of these films, would convey a different message. For unlike many of the German auteur movies of the late 1970s (whose grumpy tone they share), melancholy in its current manifestation can no longer be a reaction to an actual plight, as it lacks such experiences (decline of the "utopian," impossibility of revolution, Baader-Meinhof, etc.). Today's forms of melancholy are so nonspecific that they could also cover more far-reaching claims. One striking undertone is that of having merited something better, but of having been defrauded of it. Through the protagonists, then, the films offer an exercise in exploring the role of potential but now defeated winners. This melancholy could thus also be seen as the expression of a suppressed self-importance, another form of the "after-effects of a historical burden" that, if it were so, would be peculiar indeed.

This in turn raises a question once framed by Roland Barthes: Are there media that are reactionary "by nature, by technique"?[9] German film and television productions today provide no grounds to answer this question in the negative. On the contrary, they seem to delight in spoiling their chances of having any social relevance or consequence.

9 Roland Barthes, *The Grain of the Voice: Interviews, 1962–1980*, trans. Linda Coverdale (Evanston, IL: Northwestern University Press, 2009), 21.

Jewish Matters: Appropriation of Tradition

Did Fassbinder appropriate "Jewishness"? And why would he dare to do so? Although not Jewish himself, no other German artist since the war had explored the "Jewish question" and its history to such an extent or given it such a mass media presence—which is especially true of *BA*. In fact, a similar development can be said to have taken place among assimilated Jews at the beginning of the twentieth century. They too used appropriation to establish a new relationship with "Jewishness" or "Jewish roots." According to Gershom Scholem, a veritable cult of Eastern European Jewry broke out among German Zionists before World War I, with the Jews of Poland and Russia viewed as bearers of a pure mystery. (Walter Benjamin's "theological thinking" took off during this period.) This attitude was also at odds with the widespread contempt for those from the East among assimilated Jews. Such a fascination with submerged traditions called assimilation itself into question, and with it the values of the Enlightenment. It also marked a conflict of generations, as the "sons" raised questions that the "fathers" thought they had put firmly behind them. In *Letter to His Father*, Kafka complains that the habitual and uninspiring form of Judaism passed on to him by the addressee meant that not even religion was capable of serving as a binding tie between generations.

Scholem identified another difference that was significant for German Jews in particular. While the majority of Jewish writers (Arthur Schnitzler, Jakob Wassermann, Franz Werfel, Stefan Zweig) considered themselves Austrians or Germans, often also being great nationalists, he described a smaller, second group as men who "clearly came from foreign parts" (they included Freud, Kafka, and Benjamin): "They did not fool themselves. They knew they were German writers—but not Germans. They never cut loose from that experience and the clear awareness of being aliens, even exiles. [. . .] Closely as they knew themselves tied to the German language and its intellectual world, they never succumbed to the illusion of being at home."[1]

Döblin's position in this regard is hard to pin down. As a brief scan of his biographical background reveals, he came from an assimilated middle-class family, rarely attended synagogue, and possessed scant knowledge of the Torah. In 1912, he turned his back on religion and the Jewish community, having his children neither circumcised nor baptized. In a questionnaire in the 1920s, he gave his religion as "none," but added, "I do not want to forget: I am the child of Jewish parents."[2]

On November 5 and 6, 1923—the height of hyper-inflation, three days before Hitler's Beer Hall Putsch in Munich—there was pogrom-like, anti-Semitic violence in Berlin's Scheunenviertel neighborhood (where *BA* is set). This area was home to many Jewish emigrants who had already fled various waves of pogroms in Poland, Ukraine, Russia, and the Soviet Union, with Berlin often just a stopover on the way to the United States. The hostilities began in the queue outside the Employment Agency on Gormannstraße: right-wing agitators started a rumor that a Jewish businessman nearby had ripped off an unemployed "German." ("Strip him! Kill him!")[3]

1 Gershom Scholem, "Walter Benjamin," in *On Jews and Judaism in Crisis: Selected Essays*, ed. Werner J. Dannhauser (New York: Schocken, 1976), 191.

2 Some biographical details are taken from: Sölle, *Realisation*, 332.

Following these events, representatives of the Jewish community asked Döblin for support, promoting Zionist ideas and inviting him to Palestine. Instead, at the end of 1924, Döblin traveled to Poland. Soon after, he documented the trip in *Journey to Poland*, in which he cast an ethnological, physiognomic, sociological, and politicized eye over the country and its institutions.[4] He visited factories, left-wing newspapers, schools, and churches. Above all, however, his book gives a very detailed picture of Jewish life in cities including Vilnius, Lublin, L'viv, and Warsaw, whose Jewish quarters he explored.

Here he saw the unassimilated past of a Jewish culture that, unlike its counterpart in Berlin, had survived in almost medieval form. Döblin had the impression of seeing Jews for the first time. He was captivated by their archaic behavior and particularly fascinated by their telling family names.

But this diaspora was not the same everywhere, its character modified by regional and economic conditions. Kraków and Lodz were heavily industrialized, and life on their streets was much too elegant for Döblin's liking. In Lublin things were more rural, with Jews living in isolation and "intensely rejecting all outside things" (133). Before World War I, the territory of 1920s Poland was split between Germany, Austria, and Ukraine, and the Jewish communities were shaped by this history of occupation. In addition to this political patchwork, there were also cultural divides that crossed state boundaries. These were especially evident

3 Rainer Zilkenat, "Der Pogrom am 5. und 6. November 1923," in *Das Scheunenviertel: Spuren eines velorenen Berlins*, ed. Verein Stiftung Scheunenviertel (Berlin: Haude & Spener, 1994), 95–101.

4 Alfred Döblin, *Journey to Poland* (1925), trans. Joachim Neugroschel (London: I. B. Tauris, 1991). Page numbers are given in parentheses following citations in the text.

in Warsaw: "In the morning, a Communist scandal: outside the prayer rooms, Jewish Communists hawk gazettes with caricatures attacking 'clericalism.' The news vendors are driven away; they yell, 'Religion is the opium of the people,' fistfights break out. At a workers' kitchen, Jews have eaten and smoked on this high holiday; a brawl here too. Jews emerging from pastry shops were harassed by pious Jews" (70). "The Zionist whispers to me: 'When the Messiah comes, the laws will be abolished'" (74). "The Jewish minority demands the abolition of Sunday blue laws. They want to keep their stores open on Sundays" (59).

Conflicts within the Jewish population were also reflected in language, with Hebrew cultivated by the mostly middle-class Zionists and Yiddish by leftists, workers, and antireligious fractions. Underlying this more general diversity was a diversity of religious tradition. Döblin was particularly attentive to one rabbi, who explained, "All people have the same goal, which leads to God. There is a great land. A king rules the land. But the king cannot rule the land all by himself; he needs soldiers and generals. Those are the rebbes. How do the rebbes differ from one another? They all hold to one and the same thing. A rebbe can understand the Torah harshly or leniently. One can construe the Torah in different ways. There is a Torah of *Middas haddim*, I command, to the Torah or *Middas horakhim*, I commiserate. It's a matter of interpretation. The rebbe who understands the Torah harshly has his followers; and the one who understands it leniently has his followers. And that is what makes for the number of followers. The rebbes are pious and the sons of pious fathers. Each man chooses the rebbe with whom he sympathizes" (252–53). Döblin's feelings were mixed—fascination, revulsion, and criticism often overlapping. Some of the orthodox rites he found dreadfully atavistic, although religion could be "very beautiful"—but only concerned a single people. ("A religion must be the same for all peoples and all people, and this does not allow for a 'chosen people.' That reminds me too much of the Nazis.")[5] His relationship with Zionism was no less torn: "I reject nationalistic Zionism; I find it too European and too bourgeois."[6] "There's something gruesome about today's nationalism. I lose all desire to advocate the freedom of nations" (150).

After his journey to Poland, Döblin began learning Yiddish and worked in various Jewish organizations. In 1933 he emigrated not to Israel but, via France, to the United States, where in 1941 he joined the Catholic Church.

5 Alfred Döblin, *Briefe*, ed. Walter Muschg and Heinz Graber (Freiburg im Breisgau: Walter, 1970), 275.

6 Alfred Döblin, *Destiny's Journey* (1949), trans. Edna McCown, ed. Edgar Pässler (New York: Paragon House, 1992), 111.

Jewish Matters: *Garbage, the City, and Death*

In 1974, Fassbinder was appointed director of the Theater am Turm in Frankfurt am Main. In his application, he announced his plan to produce a play about Frankfurt. Since the theater promoted actor participation at the time, the piece was to be developed with the cast. But when the results fell short of expectations, Fassbinder ended up writing the play himself. *Garbage, the City, and Death* was produced during work on a film adaptation of Gerhard Zwerenz's novel *Die Erde ist unbewohnbar wie der Mond* (The earth is uninhabitable like the moon), from which Fassbinder borrowed certain motifs (just as Zwerenz borrowed from Döblin's *BA*).

Garbage and *Die Erde* cover the same political situation in the Frankfurt of those years: at the beginning of the 1960s, the Social Democrat city council voted for an expansive program of redevelopment in the spirit of architectural modernism. As part of this scheme, Westend, an upper-middle-class residential area built at the end of the nineteenth century and largely undamaged by the war, was declared a development zone. At the center of these plans was a plot belonging to the Rothschilds that had been acquired by the city when the family was expropriated by the Nazis in the name of "Aryanization," and that the city now refused to fully return. A partial restitution was finally agreed to in return for permission to develop more aggressively, resulting in the construction of the first high-rise tower in this quiet area, in turn encouraging further real estate speculation. The zoning plan aimed to merge smaller plots, with high-rise construction permitted on blocks above a certain size. Now existing residential buildings were systematically bought up and then run down by renting apartments to Turkish immigrants, who were referred to by left-wing students as the "fifth column" of the landlords. Where buildings could not be emptied in this way, more drastic measures were taken. It was here that "The Rich Jew" came into play, since by all accounts a key role was played in these activities by Ignatz Bubis, later chairman of the Central Council of Jews in Germany.

The reactions to *Garbage* were vehement and overwhelming, and much has been written about its complicated performance history, so I will keep this historical outline brief. Everything began with an article by Helmut Schmitz in the *Frankfurter Rundschau* on March 12, 1976, describing the play as anti-Semitic. A week later, Joachim Fest added his voice in the *Frankfurter Allgemeine Zeitung* (under the headline "Rich Jew from the Left"), accusing Fassbinder of "left-wing fascism." Another article by Fest in the same paper three weeks later bore the headline "Left-wing Trouble with the Left."

No sooner had the play been published by Suhrkamp than it was withdrawn from circulation due to the public outrage provoked by these articles. Before releasing it again, the publisher asked Fassbinder for an explanation.[1] In a statement dated "Paris, March 28, 1976," he wrote: "Under cover of this accusation certain parties are working something out whose purpose and implications I do not grasp, but that has nothing to do with me and the play. [...] And of course there are anti-Semites in this play. Unfortunately, they exist not only in this play but also, for example, in Frankfurt." The clarification provided by Fassbinder had no influence

1 These events, and those that preceded them, are documented in detail by Michael Töteberg in *Deutsch-jüdische Normalität: Fassbinders Sprengsätze* [German-Jewish normality: Fassbinder's explosive charges], ed. Elisabeth Kiderlen (Frankfurt am Main: Pflasterstrand, 1985), 21ff. The book also contains a "dialogue of the dead" between Daniel Cohn-Bendit and Fassbinder.

on the way things developed, not least because there was no new edition of the play from Suhrkamp in which it could have been published.[2]

In the years that followed, the debate on *Garbage* centered around two main issues. Firstly, undifferentiated arguments with no knowledge of the text: in most cases, such reactions were triggered by the character name The Rich Jew or the fact that at one point in the play, an old Nazi says *Judensau* (dirty Jew; literally, Jewish pig). Such knee-jerk reactions also came from representatives of Jewish organizations, which in some cases had more far-reaching repercussions. More than once, Israel's parliament, the Knesset, intervened to prevent planned productions of the play, most recently in 1985.

Secondly, the debate was characterized by inconsistencies and opportunism. Peter Zadek (to whom Fassbinder had dedicated *The Marriage of Maria Braun*), who had not found the play anti-Semitic in 1975, performed a U-turn in 1985. *Shadow of Angels* (1976), Daniel Schmid's faithful film version of *Garbage* that sparked a scandal at the Cannes Film Festival in 1977 with the departure of the Israeli delegation, was screened on other occasions with no such problems. After one of the Knesset interventions to block a production in Frankfurt, the Israeli daily newspaper *Hadashot* dryly commented that Fassbinder's play had already been shown at the Jerusalem Film Festival—without any protest.[3]

As so often in similar cases, the judicial verdict, based on close reading, possessed a subtlety that most other

2 The new edition did not appear until twenty years later, published by Verlag der Autoren. See Rainer Werner Fassbinder, "My Position on *Garbage, the City, and Death*: A Statement," in Töteberg and Lensing, *Anarchy of the Imagination*, 119.

3 Rainer Werner Fassbinder, *Der Müll, die Stadt und der Tod* (Frankfurt am Main: Verlag der Autoren, 1998), 110.

judgments lacked. In 1985, a Frankfurt court concluded: "In a play addressing the problem of anti-Semitism, artistic freedom includes the option of including anti-Semitic utterances from specific characters in the play." The ruling also said it should be taken into account "that the contested utterances are spoken on a stage, in the fictitious reality of a dramatic performance, and that the lines in question are given to characters who are depicted in an unmistakably negative light."

Incidentally, the themes and motifs dealt with in *Garbage* recur in many Fassbinder films of these years. Immediately after the play's premiere, the abovementioned *Shadow of Angels* was made, its script written by Fassbinder. Some elements also reappeared in *In a Year of 13 Moons*, whose cast also includes a Jewish property speculator in Frankfurt. The motif of destructive postwar city planning features again in *Lola* (1981), where a prostitute and a speculator are brought together by an interest in profit and a large-scale social housing project. In this case the speculator isn't Jewish but a "prole"; his distinguishing social trait is summed up by his upper-class wife: "You really are a pleb."

One direct consequence of the debate surrounding *Garbage* was the shelving of the project for a miniseries based on Gustav Freytag's *Debit and Credit* (1855), due to be made in 1977, with which Fassbinder planned to historicize the "Jewish question" in Germany in even greater depth. Fassbinder on this project:

> Taking this novel as a point of departure, one can portray the whole history of the German bourgeoisie from the mid-nineteenth century up to the rise of National Socialism—thus doing the exact opposite of what Mr. Joachim Fest does in his Hitler film, which is

> terribly reactionary and really just an attempt by a bourgeois to relieve himself of guilt. Because National Socialism is clearly based on bourgeois values—and if Fest does not portray it that way in his film, then it is because these values are still valid today. [...] In this way, we wanted to show that National Socialism was not just some random, unfortunate accident, but that it was the logical consequence of German bourgeois values. [...] And accusing me of anti-Semitism is just a clever excuse, because basically all I wanted was to show how anti-Semitism came about. [...] I don't think it is anti-Semitic to talk about which wrong moves a Jew had to make in order to survive at all. On the contrary, I think it is anti-Semitic to claim that Jews and other minorities are good and morally superior because they are minorities. [4]

In Germany, accusations of anti-Semitism often lead to a blossoming of opinion, with complexity dwindling away or being reduced to a logic of taboo breaking. Sometimes, this also serves the express purpose of avoiding discussion. In the case of *Garbage*, such discussions could have addressed the conditions of the play and of its symbolic acts. Since, to my knowledge, this never occurred, a far more general and far more interesting question arises concerning the function accorded to artistic productions in the field of "political" thought—and not only in the context of any debates on anti-Semitism they may happen to provoke.

Finally, some marginalia: the fact that anti-Semites also exist outside Fassbinder's play was something Gregor

4 Interview with Christian Brad Thomsen (1977), in Fischer, *Fassbinder über Fassbinder*, 394–95.

Gysi, an East German lawyer turned politician, experienced firsthand in 1990, during the first election campaign by the PDS (successor party to East Germany's ruling SED) after the fall of the Berlin Wall, when he too was called a "Jewish pig/dirty Jew." In the 2002 state parliament election campaign in North Rhine-Westphalia, Jürgen Möllemann, then a leading member of Germany's main liberal-economic party (FDP), organized the distribution of five million dubiously funded pamphlets combining anti-Zionist positions very similar to those of the anti-imperialist Left with widespread aversions to individuals like Michel Friedman and Ariel Sharon. Funds involved in the party donation practice of the center-right CDU (in the state of Hesse, whose largest city is Frankfurt), exposed a decade ago but yet to be explained, were declared with an ominous reference to "Jewish bequests." This can be seen as an example of a tactical "philo-Semitism" that is also cynical, bringing benefits while costing nothing—a phenomenon also dealt with by Fassbinder in *Garbage* and *13 Moons.*

Jewish Matters: Representation

> If all the Jews are bankers then how
> can they be communists too?
> —Fräulein Kost (played by Helen Vita), *Cabaret*, 1972

What may be said and showed, and by whom? And what does one call what is meant by "Jewishness"? Jewish, Jew, Judaism, Jewry, Jewish German, German Jew, German with Jewish background—all of these terms are trapped insolubly between religion, nationality, ethnicity, and "culture," and in Germany they have been particularly poisoned. Moreover, an emancipatory movement has not done one the favor of establishing a single term, even one that was previously used in a pejorative way (like "queer"), as a universally valid description. Which is why I am cautiously using scare quotes here. Compared with this wariness, Fassbinder's decision, in *Garbage, the City, and Death*, to call one of his characters "The Rich Jew" was brazen, and probably also bold. The boldness consisting in having perceived an old and still virulent stereotype as a potential source of insight.

But before new misunderstandings arise, one thing should not be overlooked here: Fassbinder was a rare thing, a German artist of the postwar period who had a strictly minoritarian perspective. Minoritarian, not identitarian. This perspective was in fact the starting point for all of the stories he told, even the most mainstream ones. And "Jewish characters" appear not only in *Garbage* but in many of his films, suggested by names or openly portrayed. In *BA* there are the two rabbis and the sausage vendor.

Beyond this, "Jewish characters" in West German feature films (until around 1985) were few and far between. Dorothea Hollstein has cited a number of cases, such as Helmut Käutner's *Black Gravel* (1961).[1] Off the top of my head—I'm not Vito Russo; exhaustive lists of representational misdemeanors are not my style—I can also think of *In Those Days* (1947), also by Käutner, and *Professor Mamlock* (1961), an East German production by Konrad Wolf.

In connection with Fassbinder, the most relevant of these films is *Black Gravel*, as it has a number of similarities with *Garbage*. Both feature a Jewish brothel owner who is called a "dirty Jew" by a Nazi; Käutner was also accused of anti-Semitism on account of his film. It is almost as if Fassbinder borrowed from Käutner for the figure of Anton Saitz in *In a Year of 13 Moons*, who besides being a real estate speculator also has a prehistory: he survived a concentration camp, traded in meat after the war, later owned a brothel (which he ran, in an exaggeration typical of Fassbinder, using "concentration camp methods").

Must this constellation be judged as anti-Semitic? Gertrud Koch did so, and more generally she accused Fassbinder of having a "problematic obsession with Jewish characters" and, ultimately, of relativizing victimhood.[2] What would she have made of the following brief scene at the beginning of *The Marriage of Maria Braun*? The setting is a soup kitchen near a train station not long after the war. In the foreground sits Maria Braun with a Red Cross nurse;

1 Dorothea Hollstein, *"Jud Süß" und die Deutschen: Antisemitische Vorurteile im nationalsozialistischen Spielfilm* (Frankfurt am Main: Ullstein, 1983), 234, 353n5.

2 Gertrud Koch, "Torments of the Flesh, Coldness of the Spirit: Jewish Figures in the Films of Rainer Werner Fassbinder," trans. Andy Spencer and Miriam Hansen, *New German Critique*, no. 38, special issue on the German-Jewish controversy (Spring–Summer 1986): 28–38.

in the background, a group of American soldiers. One of them flicks a half-smoked cigarette into the room (without thinking?) and a horde of destitute German soldiers pounces on the butt. The American turns around briefly and appears to register this humiliating scene with satisfaction. A moment later, the same soldier makes a lewd comment to his companions. Fearless as she is, Braun approaches their table and reprimands the man ("I didn't understand what you said, but you had no right to say it"), whereupon he apologizes, not in words but by giving her two packets of American cigarettes. What for him is an everyday consumer item lays the foundations for Braun's own personal economic miracle.

Although not explicitly declared as such, this soldier can also be seen as a "Jewish character." This is suggested by specific indicators, which, again, can only be mentioned with a groan: a certain facial type, large glasses with black frames (a little like Woody Allen or similarly nerdy movie characters; in Koch's listing of Jewish stereotypes in Fassbinder, this would come under: Jews as cold, resentful intellectuals). Of course, a long history of racist body classification is already embedded in this reference, meaning that it too could prompt further accusations of anti-Semitism. What would be the alternative? One could ignore the scene altogether—which would be all the easier in that it is very short and takes place in the background. But to tactfully overlook it in this way would also be to avoid the implications that give the scene its depth. In miniature format, the question of guilt is reflected here in drastic and ambivalent form: small compensation for mass murder via humiliation, small inversion of guilt via Braun's demand for politeness, second compensation via gift with cash value—in which the postwar settlement between West Germany, Israel, and the United States is, as it were, inverted.

It is unlikely that Koch's verdict on the manifest or latent anti-Semitic motifs in Fassbinder's work would have been any less harsh had she taken this scene into account. But we are dealing here with exchanges and acts of reconciliation, rather than with any kind of dubious attribution. In her essay, however, Koch was fixated on problems of representation, an approach that depends crucially on critiques of negative attributions and on the assumption that these are due to structural or conceptual defects and to malicious intent.[3]

Koch did point to possible alternatives, ways of arriving at less "problematic," less stereotypical representations. Her proposal involved more differentiated psychology. But among other things, she posited something akin to an essence of "Jewishness" and one cannot help thinking that her standards for exemplary portrayal were so high that they were almost an appeal for untouchability, for all attempts to be refrained from.[4] Which, as discussed above, has been, and in fact still is, the norm in German cinema anyway.[5]

It is easy enough to name shortcomings when one never has to deal with symbolizations or the creation of fictions

3 What were her arguments? Some excerpts: "Although Fassbinder never makes use of malicious anti-Semitic clichés in his films, there lies at the root of his creation an anti-Semitic motif [...]: The picture of the Jew as strict patriarch and man of intellect, law-abiding and austere." "As Jewish figures, Nachum and Eliser are not merged into the suffering cosmos; they remain bearers of symbols or distanced observers. Thereby, Fassbinder positions them outside of his sacrificial fantasies, guards them indeed from being falsely bound within the subjective creations of a sadomasochistic projection, but also dismisses them from history. Like most of Fassbinder's Jewish figures, those in *Berlin Alexanderplatz* also are symbols of the cold intellect which looks down upon the enslaved flesh." She also claims that "Jews" in Fassbinder's work are "anti-figures, almost abstract, as in the figure of the 'Rich Jew.'" "Latently accompanying Fassbinder's Jewish figures is a repressed anger at those who are seemingly superior, who despite extreme physical suffering still command moral superiority." And specifically about *BA* she also remarked on the prevalence of "a sexualized sadomasochistic atmosphere: The body as origin and goal of somatic perception of pain and desire is the secret theme. The world of images, which

oneself. But Koch did not even address this symbolic level at the point where it would have been central to the theme in question. This reveals a conformist side, since automatisms of preconception, irrefutability, and self-evidence are accepted and in fact taken as given. How easily a charge of anti-Semitism lures the accuser into a freewheeling or preemptive "criticality" whose logic makes it difficult not to see "anti-Semitism" at work wherever any Jewish characters feature in postwar German productions.

I do not mean to say that the approach to "Jewishness" attempted by Fassbinder is the only conceivable one, but it was an attempt (and an especially serious-minded one at that). So, in view of the paucity of "Jewish figures" in postwar German films, rather than at least acknowledging Fassbinder's exceptional efforts, the impression given was that wherever any such attempt is undertaken one must prove the ongoing virulence of old forces at all costs. For what, if not this, do such accusations of anti-Semitism boil down to?

Koch's real concern here, however, was the abovementioned and entirely justified question of what may be said and

feeds on historical extermination, is naturalized, dehistoricized in its projection onto the human body." As well as repeating these points several times over the few pages of her text, Koch also reinforced them by inclusion in multiple publications since 1985, most recently in: Gertrud Koch, *Die Einstellung ist die Einstellung: Visuelle Konstruktionen des Judentums* [The camera shot is the mindset: Visual constructions of Jewishness] (Frankfurt am Main: Suhrkamp, 1992), 250–54.

4 One of her claims in particular presents an especially desperate, hermetic inversion: "One might say that Fassbinder's anti-Semitism is a specific product of the mechanisms of repression of postwar West German history. The taboo, the ban on contact, the exclusion from everyday consciousness accumulates in Fassbinder's Jews—as a projection of the director's own coldness." Ibid., 254.

5 Apropos of refraining: In his Fassbinder book, Thomas Elsaesser defended the director against accusations of anti-Semitism, before retracting this exoneration in *German Cinema – Terror and Trauma*, doing so by playing Fassbinder's films off against those of

showed, and by whom—and the role played in this context by stereotypes. But with regard to Fassbinder's work this question was raised at the price of downgrading an allegorical approach that was highly productive within the context of the work but that is hard to translate into "identity politics." What may appear from such an identitarian position as a shocking example of negative attribution may generate a less clear-cut or threatening meaning when viewed as part of an allegorical structure.

Conceding this level of meaning to Fassbinder would have been a logical move, however, and a necessary one. Conversely, the truth also bears repeating that representation for its own sake was not among his central concerns, and "identity politics" was never a solution he took seriously.[6] What's more, Fassbinder the storyteller knew that the relationship between exemplarity and specificity can never be fully

Alexander Kluge (of all people). Kluge, he claims, dealt with the Holocaust in terms of absence, thus approaching the subject in a more appropriate manner. So how did this revaluation come about? Was it that Kluge's standing had risen to such an extent that it seemed expedient to play it off against Fassbinder's? Thomas Elsaesser, *German Cinema – Terror and Trauma: Cultural Memory since 1945* (London: Routledge, 2014).

6 Members of the German Communist Party, transgender people, Baader-Meinhof terrorists, masochists, Maoists, women, and gay people all had reason enough to complain about the ways they were "represented" by Fassbinder—and in some cases they did indeed complain.

7 How easily speaking "in one's own name" or "on one's own account" can become sugarcoated and smug is well illustrated by many "gay" or "queer" films since the 1990s and their TV series offshoots. In spite of this, Anglo-American productions since the 1980s in particular have provided many examples of subjectivizations that are both minoritarian and mass compatible. Significantly, this often happened in the field of stand-up comedy, a format based on the personal unity of writer and performer. One especially noteworthy example here is the British duo Jennifer Saunders and Dawn French, whose various TV projects packaged speaking-for-and-about-oneself and a feminist critique of gender and other orthodoxies in the form of subtle masquerade and role-play. On the same basis, a few years later in the United States, it became increasingly possible

resolved in fiction, that the specific must always be assumed to possess exemplary qualities—including the potential for failures of representation (since one cannot do everything at once).[7] Moreover, Fassbinder always treated and deployed all real-world and expressive elements as prefabricated and "ideological." Masquerade and pose were central features of his method as a whole. This allowed him to stereotype stereotypes, or even outdo them (as when he black-faced "black" actors in *The Third Generation* and *Rio das Mortes*). This, surely, is what provided the basis for Fassbinder's specific brand of realism and for the head start he gained over his peers in terms of artistic and intellectual sophistication.[8] The "Jewish issue" was the ineluctable (if rather virtual) core of

and ubiquitous to directly discuss "Jewish" matters. One particularly hilarious example is Larry David's *Curb Your Enthusiasm*: with striking frequency, the show features the easily upset sense of justice of the main character, played by David himself, or his minor worries about facing the challenges of everyday life—especially on questions of money, tipping, or the minefield of communication and behavior with lesbians, the disabled, Christians, "black" people, etc. In this case, however, this "critique" is relativized by David's own minority position—a "Jewish" one. In Germany, on the other hand, even today very often a comic effect is achieved by representatives of the social average presenting themselves as marginalized or as being sidelined by all of the world's marginalized people. German comedian Harald Schmidt has made constant use of this motif and developed it to insidious perfection. A tendency toward consolidation is also to be seen in the United States, although on an incomparably higher level. Today, few television series can do without "constructivist" arguments that were once highly advanced and only relevant in academic circles. The gay nuances in stories like *Batman* or *Sherlock Holmes*, or the homophobic overtones in some of Agatha Christie's detective novels, are now routinely included in film remakes, thus making them common knowledge. Episode 8 in season 4 of *30 Rock* included the following self-reference to "Jewish humor": "I'm sorry, are you being sarcastic? Canadians have a hard time recognizing it because we don't have a big Jewish population." In Germany, there is no feeling whatsoever for many of the fiascos of representation outlined here, not to mention the complete absence of satirical regulators like *South Park*.

8 And how many things were labeled "queer cinema" in the 1980s (and later)! The closest thing to Fassbinder's model of allegory and nonidentity-based symbolization was Stephen

Fassbinder's historiographical approach. If anywhere, then, it is in *this* respect that "Jewishness" may be problematic in his work, as he was concerned primarily not with a "Jewish" but with a "German" suffering—with the specific course of German history and an attempt to gain access to the Holocaust through storytelling, to acknowledge, express, and symbolize it. But a distinction must be made between accusations of a relativization of "Jewish" suffering and Fassbinder's attempt to guide the German culprits toward a "thou shalt suffer."

Frears's *My Beautiful Laundrette* (1985). Neither Frears nor Hanif Kureishi, who wrote the screenplay, were operating here as "concerned parties." *Laundrette* addressed Pakistani–British relations via the signifiers of deep cleaning and sexual differentiation. Meaning that instead of homosexuality or something specifically homosexual being represented, homosexuality was allegorized, beyond any sense of minority confidence building or "self-images."

Tales of a Long Night

While still in exile in California, around fifteen years after *BA*, Alfred Döblin wrote *Hamlet oder Die lange Nacht nimmt ein Ende* (or *Tales of a Long Night*, as it was published in English). The novel was completed in 1947, by which time Döblin had returned via France to West Germany. As well as being his last major work, the novel also appears as a distorting mirror and disturbing account of aesthetic positions that were already prevalent in *BA*.[1]

The plot in brief: Edward returns from the war to the south of England as an invalid. His leg has been amputated; he is a different person. Against the doctor's advice, his mother decides to nurse him at home, where his demands for "honesty" and "truth" cause fear and loathing ("obscure reproaches and accusations against Europe, against his homeland"). For Edward's father, a successful writer with a thick skin and a heavy build, his presence is a disturbance, while his mother plays her son off against her husband. The writer gets out of this tight spot by making the following proposition: instead of endlessly talking, brooding, and accusing, it would be better to tell each other stories and let these tales do the talking. This, too, will prove ineffective; the family breaks up nonetheless.

Tales of a Long Night varies central motifs and assertions from *BA*: the primacy of the vernacular, the struggle against a narcissist ego (this "ravenous," "depressed, encrusted shellfish"), storytelling as a cure ("the course of treatment they were following, an artistic one"), changes of name to

1 Alfred Döblin, *Tales of a Long Night*, trans. Robert Kimber and Rita Kimber (New York: Fromm International, 1984). Page-number references are provided in the text.

mark new leases of life or false "identities," homoerotic scenes, and an apocalyptic mood with sadomasochist overtones. And here, too, death claims the amputation of an important body part as an advance payment.

Those present now take turns to tell stories, triggering regressions all round ("We are all sinking back into the past. Everything repeats itself"). One behaves like a child, another seeks refuge in adolescent poses, the mother pursues "a cult of the body." At first, these backward transformations appear utopian, insofar as they try to approach a natural state: "She is screaming and scratching at his face. They're about to descend into the earth" (261); "I'm suffering from mole disease and have turned into a mole that tunnels under the ground and chews at the roots that push up their pretty plants" (241).

The central signifier here, however, is "imagination." It is the basis of the writer's trade and the distinctive mark of the petit bourgeois who compensates for a meager life with misjudgments. Everyone develops their own picture of everyone else and in the end all of these projections prove wrong: the son was not the Hamlet-like seeker of truth; for years, the mother suspected her husband of the gloominess that she herself was plagued by; and the Lear myth, it turns out, was a self-serving fabrication from the start.

Döblin's *Tales* contains passages written with a surprising freshness and ease—surprising because, as a German reader, one has in mind the author's depressing fate as an emigrant, as well as vague notions of the staidness of German literature after the war. But the novel soon sinks back into a heaviness that makes reading it increasingly unbearable. The characters remain blurry, the tone is agonizingly pompous, the dialogue feels hackneyed, the numerous subplots sacrifice their parabolic function to unchecked prolixity (classical mythology, legends of the saints, medieval epics, Shakespeare, Rembrandt—"Not so fast. We all have time, and especially we storytellers"; 36). A piously Christian element also does nothing to lift the general mood.

But the book is also a family novel, which, besides its dogmatism, is also what sets it furthest apart from *BA*. This family aspect culminates in an apotheosis of conjugal love, with a conclusion for which the term "melodrama" is an understatement. Salvation comes literally at the last moment, and only for this one moment: as the writer lies dying, his wife, once confident and elegant, now totally gone to pieces, finds her way back to him ("She prayed and implored. […] Alice talked to Gordon for the first time. For the first time Gordon talked to Alice. They left nothing unsaid"; 475).

It is not very often that narrative texts trigger such strong aversion. Bewilderment and sadness are joined by disgust and a great uneasiness, none of which can be explained purely in terms of technical weaknesses. Instead, they are an emotional response to the attitudes on show here. Some samples: "There you have an image of our ravenous, insatiable ego. […] 'I' can only count to one. It is never part of a chord. […] But in the old legend, the god Mod knew better what had to be done. No attempts at reform. Just wipe the beast out and clear the way for recovery" (236). "She clung to this stranger with her utmost passion. She practically clawed him to pieces. She gave herself up to him as a building yields to a bomb, apartments, stairways, walls, all crashing down into the cellar. She made a burnt offering of herself" (451).

In the last third of the book, the banker Raymond enters Alice's life as a "dastardly" man of action and says, "Yes, we have to reduce man to the animal. We have to bring him to the truth by relieving him of his brain. […] He 'thinks' to protect himself from the truth. That is the birth of idealism. […] The next step is not one that everybody is willing to take. Most people cling to their illusions. It takes courage to break through to the truth. But before that, of course, comes disgust, insight into the lie and disgust for it. […] The breakthrough takes you into an ice-cold realm." Alice whispers, "The route to bestiality." Raymond: "The route to the truth. Rousseau minus the sentimentality." Alice: "Make an animal of me!" Raymond: "Should I kill you then?" "Fear ran through him" (446–47).

Having not gotten herself killed after all, Alice, the fallen wife and mother, wonders to herself:

> For men are blind and foolish. They don't see that you can do things this way or that way, and whichever way you choose is all one. We're all lost one way or another, and we let ourselves be duped with pleasure and society and a high standard of living. The banker is right: we should hit anyone in the face who claims there is something we can hold on to. And so all the questions about guilt and responsibility are pointless. For we can do whatever we like. We can make war. Why not? We are smoke, a ball to be tossed about. And we can be rulers, too, tyrants, beasts. (451)

The book's view of history is thus as follows: "[Edward:] 'So we're left with history minus human beings!' [Gordon:] 'Minus so-called free and independent actions'" (126).

Burnt offering, reducing to the animal, wiping out the beast—the book certainly cannot be said to lack crassness or dubious passages. But although these words are clearly attributed to fictional characters, it is also clear that Döblin did not deploy any kind of distancing mechanism. In view of this novel, Adorno's remark about "the dark drives of the intelligentsia before 1933" and Derrida's charge that Benjamin's text on violence somehow anticipated National Socialism and the Holocaust can both be applied without hesitation to Döblin. Except—and this hugely increases the sense of unease—that *Tales of a Long Night* was written not before 1933, but shortly after 1945. Meaning that the book was produced at the same time as Thomas Mann's *Doctor Faustus.* And the similarity between the two novels goes further: besides the common theme of the artist, they were both reactions to World War II, and they both use familiar myths to overdetermine the narrative. In retrospect, however, *Doctor Faustus* appears by far the more accomplished work. Not only did Mann's ironic method prove the more effective instrument, but his choice and treatment of references display a rigor and sophistication totally lacking in Döblin.

The decisive difference, however, is that *Doctor Faustus* aimed, among other things, to shed light on the intellectual precursors of National Socialism and that the figures of thought that his attention focuses on are precisely those that Döblin was not willing to relinquish even after the war (archaic references, "anti-humanist" ruthlessness, barbarism). What's more, the "bourgeois" author—what designated Mann as Döblin's artistic antagonist—also included a critique of his own questionable affinities as they appear in *Reflections of a Nonpolitical Man* (1918).[2]

This is something Döblin did not do. On the contrary, he wanted to confirm once again, in the strongest possible terms, a worldview described by Dorothee Sölle: "There is

2 A concluding remark in chapter 28 of *Doctor Faustus* reads like a resume: "Today we see, of course, that it was the mistake of our civilization to have practiced all too magnanimously this respect and forbearance. For we found after all that the opposite side met us with sheer impudence and the most determined intolerance." Mann, *Doctor Faustus*, 284.

no redemption; only in extreme suffering and death is a mythical union achieved with nature."[3] Damage was done as a result: this "storytelling in the aftermath of disaster" became a disaster in its own right.

Nonetheless, even in this novel, Döblin comes across as one of the more versatile and substantial German writers of his time. But in view of its antihumanist stance and its reliance on "dark urges," it is a double irony of German literary history that it was not printed until 1956—in socialist East Germany.

3 Sölle, *Realisation*, 306.

Exhibiting a Movie

Can a TV series be exhibited in an art space? In 2007, Kunst-Werke Institute for Contemporary Art (KW) in Berlin tried to do this with Fassbinder's *BA*. The show included film stills, facsimiles of the paperback edition of *BA* with Fassbinder's annotations and cuts, and excerpts from tape recordings of Fassbinder dictating the script (as seen in his episode of *Germany in Autumn*, 1978). The central element, however, was a large U-shaped structure made of plywood representing a "Berlin backyard." Here, behind fourteen milky windows, the individual episodes of the series were shown in small screening rooms, in parallel, over and over. As this approach made clear, the focus was on duplicating the visual source material to the greatest possible degree. Accordingly, the full fifteen hours of film were also shown in an additional screening room, this time in chronological order. And there were more screens dotted about the gallery showing selected highlights. In spite of this abundance, however, the basic assumption was that no one would really ever sit down and watch the entire series.

In other words, visitors were confronted with an approach to presenting art that was strikingly careless in its inappropriateness, with higher-order aspects pushed to the fore. Art institutions with their specific distribution of meaning are now considered an adequate place to host exhibitions of moving images. More generally, it seems that film practices once considered experimental or avant-garde can now find a place only in the context of art institutions. And it goes without saying that an extra-long movie can also be blithely presented in such a context.

One problem did remain, however, and the exhibition approached it with agreeable openness. It concerns the institution's self-image and the value system on which it is based. What began as a critique of the white cube (as in the writings of Brian O'Doherty) has, paradoxically enough, contributed to a huge increase in the value of that same institution. This critique of the neutrality of the art space has now been totally internalized, with an implicit "criticality" now the very basis of its meaning. The art space absorbs the content of artistic productions, lending them an aura of untouchability in return. This has led to a new status quo, new commonplaces, and distinct forms of whitewashing and stupidity. The stupidity results from the self-satisfaction with which art institutions operate, their belief in their own license to frame the creation of meaning however they please. On the other hand, as another effect of these same conditions, paying attention to a "fine hanging" or "installation" is now a staple of the aesthetic repertoire. It is equally natural to turn one's attention to the history of the exhibition space, its material qualities, the socioeconomic setting and its implications, one's own forms of presentation, and thus the curatorial act itself.

In the case of *BA*, however, the work in question was depleted and taken out of context in every imaginable way. Narrative and the function of fictionality should of course have constituted the primary subject matter and context here. Though the show superficially paid tribute to the importance and prestige of narrative, precisely this aspect was in fact largely ignored. Instead, *BA* was parodied in the form of an "installation," drawn out into a network of meanings: that of Fassbinder as celebrity and trademark, and that of the art institution itself, with the gallery taking credit for turning the series into an "exhibitable" object. Incidentally, this also addressed a question often raised in connection with twentieth-century cinema concerning its status as art, providing an answer in the form of a circular argument: film can be art, if and as soon as it is put on show in an art space.

This presentation of *BA* at KW, then, was merely the latest way of not actually engaging with the series. It would have been possible, for example, to at least use the catalogue to respond to the film's half-hearted reception in Germany. Instead, a badly designed doorstop of a coffee-table book was produced that shirked this challenge by printing blown-up stills and a facsimile of a workbook originally published in 1980 to accompany the TV debut of the series. Ultimately, the fact of the non-reception of *BA* in Germany was actually consolidated here, using forms of showiness and presumption that are available in the art context. The fact that the exhibition was also aimed at an American audience (the show was slated to travel to MoMA PS1 in New York) made it appear all the more simpleminded in view of the far greater engagement with Fassbinder's oeuvre in the United States.

Index

30 Rock 158n21, 207n7

Achternbusch, Herbert 51, 105, 175n1
Adorno, Theodor W. 59–60, 102, 123, 132, 179, 212
Ali: Fear Eats the Soul (*Angst essen Seele auf*) 11n3, 112
Antonioni, Michelangelo 84–85, 99

Badiou, Alain 148, 158
Baer, Harry 14n6, 126n19
Bakhtin, Mikhail 88–89, 98n20, 104
Barthes, Roland 62, 109n35, 111–13, 134, 188
Baudry, Jean-Louis 75
Bazin, André 59n22, 186
Bellour, Raymond 66
Benjamin, Walter 41, 46, 58, 62, 75, 79, 121–22, 124–25, 148, 159n24, 161, 164n1, 189, 190, 213
Benveniste, Émile 93n18
Bergman, Ingmar 52n10, 61, 105
Bertolucci, Bernardo 52n10, 84–85, 99
Black Gravel 202
Bockmayer, Walter 144n9, 175n1
Brecht, Bertolt 48–53, 73, 108, 111–13, 119n8, 134, 161, 163
Bresson, Robert 50, 71, 76
Brüggemann, Heinz 54–55, 58

Cabaret 52n9, 201
Carstensen, Margit 74, 149
Caven, Ingrid 14n6, 36, 113n2, 126, 165
Coffee Shop, The 27, 63n27, 73
Cohn-Bendit, Daniel 196n1
Counterfeiters, The 67
Crimp, Douglas 12n5, 63n28, 128n21
Curb Your Enthusiasm 207n7

Deadwood 183n5
Death of Maria Malibran, The 109n35
Decision, The 108, 134, 163
Deleuze, Gilles 66–68, 75–76, 105–6

Derrida, Jacques 93n18, 124–25, 213
Despair 74, 175n1
Doctor Faustus 122–23, 125n18, 213
Dostoyevsky, Fyodor M. 81, 89, 98, 104
Düringer, Annemarie 27, 33, 74

Eco, Umberto 87n10
Effi Briest 8, 11n3
Eisenstein, Sergei M. 49, 55, 66, 71
Elsaesser, Thomas 12n5, 48n5, 71n7, 128n21, 139n2, 176n2, 205n5

Far from Heaven 183n5
Flaubert, Gustave 46, 81, 113
Fleißer, Marieluise 137, 163n1
Foucault, Michel 76, 93n18, 109n35
French, Dawn 206n7
Freud, Sigmund 7, 14n6, 75, 107, 143–45, 146, 153–54, 156, 190

Garbage, the City, and Death (*Der Müll, die Stadt und der Tod*) 129–30, 132, 195–200, 201–2
Germany in Autumn (*Deutschland im Herbst*) 113n2, 215
Gide, André 46, 67–68
Godard, Jean-Luc 50–51, 52n10, 55, 84–85, 100n24, 166
Gogol, Nikolai 98
Goldoni, Carlo 27, 63n27, 73
Grafe, Frieda 61n25
Gramsci, Antonio 86n9
Grass, Günter 58
Greenberg, Clement 60
Guattari, Félix 69, 75

Hamburger, Käte 66
Haynes, Todd 183n5
Hitchcock, Alfred 105, 139–41
Hitler: A Film from Germany 52nn9–10, 175n1, 182n4
Huillet, Danièle 50, 71, 132n31

Iden, Peter 55n13, 63n27
In a Year of 13 Moons (*In einem Jahr mit 13 Monden*) 27, 37, 55n13, 70, 73, 112, 126, 129, 130–31, 134–35, 144n9, 148, 151n18, 198, 200, 202

Journey to Poland 191–93
Joyce, James 81–82

Katzelmacher 112
Käutner, Helmut 202
Kippenberger, Martin 15n7, 115n5, 178n3
Kluge, Alexander 50–51, 206n5
Koch, Gertrud 202–5
Kristeva, Julia 62
Kusturica, Emir 15n7

Lacan, Jacques 93n18, 142, 145, 146–47, 148, 157
Laffay, Albert 66
Lamprecht, Günter 19, 33, 106
Lemke, Klaus 51n8
Lili Marleen 112, 133n31, 180
Lola 9, 112, 130n26, 198
Lola Montès 72n9
Love Is Colder Than Death (*Liebe ist kälter als der Tod*) 112, 129n24, 163
Mad Men 183n5
Mann, Thomas 73, 81, 107–8, 122–23, 125n18, 213
Marcuse, Ludwig 57n19
Marriage of Maria Braun, The (*Die Ehe der Maria Braun*) 112, 131n28, 181, 197, 202–3
Martha 72
Merchant of Four Seasons, The (*Händler der vier Jahreszeiten*) 11n3
Mother Küsters Goes to Heaven (*Mutter Küsters' Fahrt zum Himmel*) 112
My Beautiful Laundrette 208n8

Negri, Antonio 172

Ophüls, Max 72n9
Out 1 52n10
Overcoat, The 98

Paludes 67
Pascal, Roy 82
Pasolini, Pier Paolo 50, 51, 52n9, 67–68, 82–87, 99, 105–7, 109
Poor Folk 98
Praunheim, Rosa von 51, 105
Proust, Marcel 45, 101–2, 113n3

Querelle 8, 70, 74, 80n2, 106n31

Raben, Peer 160n25

Rio das Mortes 9, 165n3, 207
Rivette, Jacques 52n10
Robbe-Grillet, Alain 50
Rouch, Jean 51n7

Salem m'Barek Mohammed Mustafa, El Hedi ben 8
Satan's Brew (*Satansbraten*) 8, 62n26
Saunders, Jennifer 206n7
Scenes from a Marriage 52n10
Shadow of Angels 197–98
Schediwy, Fritz 21
Schmid, Daniel 197
Schmitt, Carl 121n9, 124, 161
Scholem, Gershom 189–90
Schroeter, Werner 51, 55n13, 105, 109n35
Schygulla, Hanna 25, 36
Sebald, W. G. 123–24
Silverman, Kaja 12n5, 128n21, 138n1
Sirk, Douglas 10n3, 65, 164, 183n5
Smith, Jack 51n8, 105
Sölle, Dorothee 127n20, 190n2, 213–14
Sontag, Susan 138
South Park 207n7
Spitzer, Leo 81
Stationmaster's Wife, The (*Bolwieser*) 11n3
Stein, Peter 63n27
Straub, Jean-Marie 50, 71, 132n31
Syberberg, Hans-Jürgen 51, 52nn9–10, 175n1, 182n4

Theweleit, Klaus 151
Third Generation, The (*Die Dritte Generation*) 27, 70, 112, 181, 207
To Catch a Thief 139–40
Torquato Tasso 63n27, 148
Trier, Lars von 186n7

Valentin, Barbara 26
Van Vechten, Carl 171
Veronika Voss (*Die Sehnsucht der Veronika Voss*) 8, 131n28
Vita, Helen 32, 33, 201
Vološinov, Valentin 87–90

Warhol, Andy 51n8, 75, 105, 106n31
Whity 7, 9
Wire, The 100n23

Manfred Hermes is a writer based in Berlin. He is a frequent contributor to international art journals, magazines, newspapers, and exhibition catalogues. His previous publications include the monographs *Ull Hohn* and *Martin Kippenberger.*

Manfred Hermes
Hystericizing Germany: Fassbinder, Alexanderplatz

Published by Sternberg Press

Translation: Nicholas Grindell
Editor: Max Bach
Proofreading: Niamh Dunphy
Design: HIT
Cover illustration: Enrico David
Printing: BUD Potsdam

ISBN 978-3-95679-004-1

First published as
Deutschland hysterisieren: Fassbinder, Alexanderplatz
© 2011 b_books, Berlin

The translation of this work was funded by Geisteswissenschaften International – Translation Funding for Humanities and Social Sciences from Germany, a joint initiative of the Fritz Thyssen Foundation, the German Federal Foreign Office, the collecting society VG WORT, and the Börsenverein des Deutschen Buchhandels (German Publishers & Booksellers Association).

Sternberg Press
Caroline Schneider
Karl-Marx-Allee 78
D-10243 Berlin
www.sternberg-press.com